FRANCIS ASBURY

10-00

FRANCIS ASBURY

L. C. Rudolph

Abingdon Press

NASHVILLE

Acknowledgments

The librarians of Drew University, of Garrett Theological Seminary, and of the Association of Methodist Historical Societies are due special thanks. They gave me help beyond any call of duty. In addition to bibliographical aid, the staff of the library at The Methodist Publishing House extended many personal courtesies during my labors there. My colleagues in the faculty and staff of Louisville Presbyterian Seminary have given both encouragement and concrete assistance.

L. C. RUDOLPH

Contents

Abbreviations

JLFA   *The Journal and Letters of Francis Asbury,* ed. by Elmer T. Clark, J. Manning Potts, and Jacob S. Payton. Nashville: Abingdon Press, 1958.

        Vol. I: The Journal, 1771-1793.
        Vol. II: The Journal, 1794-1816.
        Vol. III: The Letters.

        Since Asbury often combined the events of several days in one *Journal* entry—and since it is not always possible to determine the exact day on which he was writing—all references in the footnotes are given as the *entry* date in this edition of the *Journal.*

HAM   *The History of American Methodism.* 3 vols. Nashville: Abingdon Press, 1964.

LJW   *The Letters of the Rev. John Wesley, A.M.,* ed. by John Telford. 8 vols. London: Epworth Press, 1931.

After the first full source identification, all footnote references will be made in abbreviated form. To expand an abbreviated reference the reader may refer to the alphabetical bibliography at the back of the book.

PART I
Getting Established

1
TO AMERICA

Francis Asbury had no bed on board ship. His friends had raised money to provide him two blankets; these he spread on the ship's bare planks to sleep the fifty-three nights of his voyage. Even to the bones of a man of twenty-six, the nights were cold and the floor unyielding. "I found it hard to lodge on little more than boards. I want faith, courage, patience, meekness, love. When others suffer so much for their temporal interests, surely I may suffer a little for the glory of God, and the good of souls." [1] Further, the crossing was rough.

For three days I was very ill with the seasickness; and no sickness I ever knew was equal to it. [2]

The wind blowing a gale, the ship turned up and down, and from side to side, in a manner very painful to one that was not accustomed to sailing; but when Jesus is in the ship all is well. [3]

[1] September 15, 1771; JLFA, I, 5.
[2] September 4, 1771; JLFA, I, 4.
[3] September 15, 1771; JLFA, I, 5.

His determination never seemed to falter. When his seasickness eased enough so he could focus his eyes on print, he studied. Every Sunday that he was able to stand on the deck he preached to the ship's passengers and crew. One Sunday when the wind was so strong he could not stand unaided he fixed his back against the mizzenmast and preached all the same. He dared not be hopeful that this preaching found its mark, but the Lord's day would not pass without preaching if he could help it. "Whilst they will hear, I will preach, as I have opportunity." [4]

John Wesley urged every Methodist preacher to keep a journal or diary as an aid in self-discipline. Francis Asbury had been a Methodist preacher without a journal for five years, but now, on the ship from England to America, he began keeping his daily record.

> I will set down a few things that lie on my mind. Whither am I going? To the New World. What to do? To gain honour? No, if I know my own heart. To get money? No: I am going to live to God, and to bring others so to do. In America there has been a work of God: some moving first amongst the Friends, but in time it declined; likewise by the Presbyterians, but amongst them also it declined. The people God owns in England, are the Methodists. The doctrines they preach, and the discipline they enforce, are, I believe, the purest of any people now in the world. The Lord has greatly blessed these doctrines and this discipline in the three kingdoms: they must therefore be pleasing to him. If God does not acknowledge me in America, I will soon return to England. I know my views are upright now; may they never be otherwise.[5]

Who was this young Englishman with his eyes set so firmly on America? Francis Asbury once recorded his own vital statistic.

> I was born in Old England, near the foot of Hampstead Bridge, in the parish of Handsworth, about four miles from Birmingham, in

[4] September 29, 1771; JLFA, I, 6.
[5] September 12, 1771; JLFA, I, 4-5.

Staffordshire, and according to the best of my after-knowledge on the 20th or 21st day of August, in the year of our Lord 1745.[6]

He was the son of a skilled farmer and gardener named Joseph Asbury, who worked for the two wealthiest families in the parish. His mother was Elizabeth Rogers Asbury, a literate and sensitive person. Religion was early a lively matter in his home. After his sister Sarah died, his mother was deeply shocked; religion was her continuing consolation. England teemed with religious societies; the evangelical Anglican preachers such as Stillingfleet, Bagnall, and Venn urged the founding of these intensely pious groups. Elizabeth Asbury's house was open to them all. Joseph was a practicing churchman but hardly zealous for the societies.

Since Francis was now their only child, Joseph and Elizabeth Asbury were especially interested in his education. They sent him to school early, so that he was reading the Bible by the time he was seven. They would have been glad for him to press on as a scholar. However, the venture into formal education failed. Francis was intensely serious and introspective. His fellow students counted him a religiously melancholy son of a religiously eccentric mother, and the schoolmaster was a heavy disciplinarian who found no way to relate to this boy. Francis dropped out of school before he was twelve with little to show for his labor except an aversion to formal education. He never went back.

His parents next arranged for Francis to serve as an apprentice, a sort of on-the-job training to be a business employee or craftsman. In his first apprenticeship he discovered that he was pious but the household was not. That arrangement did not last very long. The second apprenticeship was with a kind and pious craftsman who treated Francis well.

There is no solid evidence indicating the trade to which he was apprenticed. There are opinions that he worked as a button maker, a buckle maker, a leather worker, or as a metal worker at a forge.

[6] July 16, 1792; JLFA, I, 720.

His only word is that he "wrought" at this business about six years and a half, "and in the family was treated more like a son or an equal than an apprentice." [7] That might have been the end of the story. An apprentice normally learned a trade and practiced it usefully but without wide recognition until he died. An apprentice normally left no writings and made small personal mark in the world's history.

Francis did not complete his training and enter life as a craftsman because his zeal for evangelical religion burned in him until it came to determine his life's work. As a mere lad his interests had been deeply religious; he was reared in a home atmosphere charged with piety and straining for religious fulfillment. His parents were Church of England people, but the Church of England was not exactly the same in all its parts. The parts of the Church of England which Francis and his mother liked best were the evangelical or revivalistic ones. They appreciated preaching which called for revolution in life and did it with fervency. They found satisfaction in the intensive fellowship of the visibly converted. When their own rector provided little of this intense religion, they visited the West Bromwich church, where personal evangelism was featured and enthusiasm encouraged. Near the beginning of Asbury's second apprenticeship "God sent a pious man, not a Methodist, into our neighbourhood, and my mother invited him to our house; by his conversation and prayers, I was awakened before I was fourteen years of age." [8]

Since the Asburys were interested in evangelistic preaching and intensive fellowship of the converted, it was inevitable that they should hear of the Methodists. The Methodists excelled in both. Methodists were not all of one kind; Francis Asbury contacted the Wesleyan or Arminian Methodists. He heard reports of them at Wednesbury. It was a plain case of love at first sight.

Francis liked the way the Methodists preached, so personally

---

[7] July 16, 1792; JLFA, I, 721.
[8] July 16, 1792; JLFA, I, 721; cf. 44, 123-25.

and confidently. He liked the way they prayed, with feeling and without the use of a book. He liked the way they sang, with melody and fervor. He liked what he saw of the life and loyalty of the members. Soon he began to "meet class" with the Methodists at Bromwich Heath and to "meet in band" with the Methodists at Wednesbury.

It is well to remember that these Methodist societies, like the evangelical societies already mentioned, were overshadowed by the state church. There was no organic link between Methodism and the Church of England but the religious life of the Methodists assumed a Church of England. Their meetings were not held at the hour of regular church services but were additional. Methodist society members were normally expected to support the Church of England by taxes, to attend the Church of England services using the *Book of Common Prayer,* to receive the sacraments only from the Church of England clergy, and to be faithful members of their Church of England parish. Francis Asbury was now a Methodist society member in the Church of England.

Being a Methodist opened some wonderful opportunities to Francis Asbury. The plan seemed to suit him exactly. He had been "awakened" to an uneasiness about his own salvation; in this Methodist fellowship he became sure that his sins were forgiven and that he was in saving relationship with God. He had found religious activity the chief interest of his life but lacked the university training to be a Church of England clergyman; in this Methodist fellowship he could be a preacher without a university training.

John Wesley was the director of the Wesleyan Methodists. He had been at work for twenty years preaching and forming societies to help Church of England people actually to live the Christian life. The work had grown large. So Wesley developed a plan of using unordained men, gifted Methodist society members, as preachers. Several such preachers would work under the supervision of an "assistant" to John Wesley, and Wesley would superintend the whole enterprise. The Methodist societies were growing fast and needed preachers, some to be local preachers for groups near their home and some to be traveling preachers making an endless round of the classes or societies.

Though Francis Asbury was very young, he was soon trying his hand at preaching. He spoke to some neighbors who met regularly at or near his own house. First he announced hymns and read scripture and led in prayer; then he "exhorted," that is, he urged the people to apply the scripture passage or the sermon to their own lives. Then he preached in the vicinity as he was invited. All this was very exciting: "Behold me now a local preacher!" Before long he was preaching "generally, three, four, and five times a week" even while still working as an apprentice.[9]

In 1766 he had his first appointment as a traveling Methodist preacher in Staffordshire. Other appointments followed year by year in Bedfordshire, Colchester, and Wiltshire. He wrote home hoping his parents would adjust quickly and happily to his new work.

> I love my parents and friends but I love my God better and his service.[10]

> You may send me a letter when you can, and let me know how you do. I have much work on my hands and am put to it for time to do what I want.[11]

There was no doubt that Francis Asbury had found his place. He seems never to have questioned his call to the occupation of traveling preacher. Nothing dared to get in the way of this calling. If there were limitations, he simply refused them. As one biographer says it, Methodism was his wife and child.[12]

Being a traveling Methodist preacher was not easy; it took both strength and courage. The Methodists preached to miners and fac-

[9] July 16, 1792; JLFA, I, 722.
[10] October 26, 1768; JLFA, III, 4.
[11] November 6, 1769; JLFA, III, 7.
[12] George P. Mains, *Francis Asbury* (New York: Eaton and Mains, 1909), p. 119.

tory workers who had not been to church in years. There were hoodlums in those crowds who did not want preaching to be easy for anybody. They organized gangs to heckle the preachers or even to beat them. Sometimes the regular Anglican preacher and the police in a town had no love for the Methodists and did not mind seeing them suffer just for the crowd's amusement.

Being a traveling Methodist preacher took brains, too. Only a few in the congregations were well educated, but no offense must be given to those few. If the preacher expected to hold the shifting congregation together at all he must make his points sharp, clear, and moving. Sometimes the Methodist preacher was thrown into contest with regular university-trained clergy who would accuse him of being an ignorant parish breaker. Francis Asbury faced all this with no more than six years of formal schooling; those sermons were tough to prepare. He said: "I wonder some times how anyone will sit to hear me, but the Lord covers my naked-ness with his power." [13] But then he did not rely on providence alone. He got a lot of help from John Wesley. If Wesley accepted lay preachers, it must be added that he did not want ignorant lay preachers. Wesley published books—over one hundred titles dur-ing his life—and he kept the preachers under pressure to read, to study, to learn, to teach. Francis Asbury knew enough to read and write; now he had the material and the motive to get on with his education. His nose was always in a book, and he was soaking up learning at a great rate to compensate for lost time.

All the while he was so excited about his work it was hard for him to stay within the bounds of discipline. Even as a fledgling preacher he kept seeing places where changes in preachers and practice should be made. His supervisor did not appreciate so much advice and wrote him suggesting that he just do his own work without "gazing all around." [14]

In spite of hard lessons from books and from people, he must

[13] To his parents, October 26, 1768; JLFA, III, 4.
[14] May 23, 1766; JLFA, III, 10.

have done pretty well. Every year he was again named as a travel-ing preacher. In 1771 all the English Methodist preachers met with Mr. Wesley in conference at Bristol. During the meeting Wesley said, "Our brethren in America call aloud for help. Who are willing to go over and help them?" [15] Of the five who volun-teered, Francis Asbury and Richard Wright were chosen to go. Asbury had been thinking hard about visiting America. Now John Wesley was willing to risk sending him as a Methodist rep-resentative in America. It would be hard to imagine a more con-vinced and zealous disciple.

Within three weeks Asbury had taken leave of his parents, visited his friends on the circuits he had served, and prepared to sail from Bristol. He said: "When I came to Bristol I had not one penny of money." [16] The local Methodists raised enough to buy him clothes and give him ten pounds for the trip. The ship sailed on September 4. Some former parishioners wrote to his mother: "We have heard that your son is going, or is gone, to America. . . . We can scarce believe he is so mad." [17]

Neither high seas nor contrary opinions in any way cooled the zeal of Asbury.

O that we may always walk worthy of the vocation wherewith we are called! When I came near the American shore, my very heart melted within me, to think from whence I came, where I was going, and what I was going about.[18]

The day of the landing at Philadelphia was October 27, 1771.

[15] 1771 Minutes, in *Minutes of the Methodist Conferences from the First, Held in London, by the Late Rev. John Wesley, A.M., in the Year 1744* (London: John Mason, 1862), I (1744-1797), 98.

[16] August 7, 1771; JLFA, I, 4.

[17] August 27, 1771; JLFA, III, 9-10.

[18] October 27, 1771; JLFA, I, 7.

2
MEETING THE
AMERICAN METHODISTS

Francis Asbury was not the first Wesleyan Methodist in America. Wesley's work had now been growing in the British Isles for thirty years. Among the English and Irish settlers who had come to America were several who had been in Methodist societies back home. Some had been local preachers before moving to the New World.

There was one early cluster of Methodists in New York. Here the key man was Philip Embury, who had been a local preacher in Ireland. When he moved to New York he did not immediately carry on as a preacher. It took the shrill urging of his neighbor and cousin Barbara Heck to get him started; she said unless something was done all of them would be slipping away into hell. So the Methodist preaching in New York began at Embury's house. As the congregation grew they moved to a rented room, to a rigging loft, and then to their own stone building called Wesley Chapel.

One reason for the good progress of the New York society was the work of Captain Thomas Webb.[1] He was a most colorful character, a one-eyed British army officer now retired from active duty and with time on his hands. Webb had become an enthusiastic Methodist in England and he intended to be one in America. Therefore he joined Embury's group. Webb preached; he gave money; he got other people to give money; he went to Philadelphia, Delaware, and New Jersey organizing Methodist groups; he bullied the English Methodists into sending some traveling preachers to America as missionaries. It would be hard to imagine early American Methodist history without him.

There was another early cluster of Methodists in the south. These were members of the societies served by Robert Strawbridge, mostly in Maryland. Strawbridge was a Methodist local preacher who had come over from Ireland. He was not really under the direction of Wesley; for a long time Wesley did not even know he was there. He was hardly under the direction of the Methodist brethren at New York and Philadelphia, although Captain Webb came down to visit at least once. Indeed, there is an involved argument whether the Methodist society founded by Strawbridge is not really the first in America.[2] Strawbridge saw a need for Methodist preaching, so he delivered it. In spite of the fact that he was a married man with a family to support, he gave most of his time to riding a wide circuit of preaching places in Maryland, Delaware, Pennsylvania, and Virginia and to training some young lay preachers to help him in the work. Since it seemed to him that the Methodist people in his societies needed to have the sacraments, and it was difficult to find any ordained Church of England clergyman to serve them, he simply administered the Lord's Supper and baptism himself, though he was not ordained.

Francis Asbury was not even the first official Methodist missionary to America. Wesley had heard the call from the brethren in America before and had sent help; Richard Boardman and Joseph Pilmoor arrived in 1769. They had been alternating between New

---

[1] See Frank Baker, "Captain Thomas Webb, Pioneer of American Methodism," *Religion in Life*, XXXIV (1965), 406-21.

[2] HAM, I, 74-80.

York and Philadelphia every few months for two years and serving several preaching points in the country besides. Boardman was in charge and decided when the two missionaries would switch places.

All in all, it was a loose and wobbly structure, this Methodism in America. Both Pilmoor and Boardman were working almost entirely in New York and Philadelphia. Pilmoor was complaining that Wesley was not sending much help and that Boardman was moving him around too often.[3] Captain Webb was probably more influential than either missionary and was hardly taking direction from them. Robert Strawbridge in Maryland was not calling for help or advice from anybody. He was going his independent way with impressive success.

So Francis Asbury expected to find some beginnings of Methodism in America; Methodists were waiting for him at Philadelphia in the fall of 1771. They even had a large building in that city. A German Reformed congregation had gone bankrupt constructing a church for over two thousand pounds and so had to sell it at great loss at auction. At the auction a mentally deficient son of a prominent family had been high bidder at 700 pounds. The family did not want either to have the church or to admit the son's mental deficiency, so they quietly sold the building to the Methodists for 650 pounds. Pilmoor reports this boon for the Methodists and marvels, "How wonderful are the Dispensations of Providence! Surely the very hairs of our heads are all numbered."[4] It was Pilmoor who preached in the church the night Asbury and Wright arrived. Asbury was impressed with the church and with the warm welcome. He was not impressed with the discipline among Methodists at either Philadelphia or New York.

It was in New York, with the society at Wesley Chapel, that he was to work first. So he traveled there early in November, preaching as he went. Boardman was working in New York too. Asbury was unhappy about having two Methodist preachers living in one city at the same time. The Wesley Chapel membership was not

[3] Joseph Pilmoor, Manuscript Journal, the Historical Center Library, Old St. George's, Philadelphia. Transcription by Cornelius Hudson, pp. 80, 129.

[4] Ibid., p. 16.

large, though the size of the evening congregations was often impressive. There was preaching on Tuesday evening, on Thursday evening, and twice on Sunday. The preacher was to "meet the class" on Wednesday evening, a time when the faithful members in full relation to the society were to search and improve their Christian lives. Even if they added preaching on Friday evening, exhortation on Saturday evening, and preaching certain mornings at five o'clock in Wesley's fashion, this did not seem to Asbury to be enough work to excuse the presence of two preachers.

Two things may be said about Asbury's concern. First, it is hardly fitting to speak of American "cities" at the time Asbury began his ministry. New York was a town of just over twenty thousand; its slightly larger and more prestigious urban neighbor, Philadelphia, was a hard two-day trip away by wagon. Baltimore, rising center of Methodism, did not number five thousand until 1773; the city had no pavements, no police, no street lights, and was known for mudholes which made the main streets almost impassible in autumn and spring.[5] Second, only some 3 percent of the population of the colonies lived in towns over eight thousand. Asbury was concerned about getting the preachers out into the country where the people were living on their farms. So when he was in New York he complained about the preachers' staying in the city. He set up more preaching points around the city and spent more time riding out in the country to "show them the way."[6] This was his pattern, this "gazing around" over all the population and all the religious enterprise of the land which had brought him the reprimand of his superior in England.

Also, when he was in New York, he pressed the people hard about their discipline: they were allowing nonmembers to attend love feasts and society meetings which should be for members only; they were not strict enough about excluding disorderly persons; their zeal as Methodists was not keen enough. Asbury did not want

---

[5] James E. Armstrong, *History of the Old Baltimore Conference from the Planting of Methodism in 1773 to the Division of the Conference in 1857* (Baltimore: King Brothers, 1907), p. 4.

[6] November 21, 1771; JLFA, I, 10.

people flirting with Methodism unless they wanted all the restraints of holy living.

Some of the early results of Asbury's strong will are plain. New circuits were established in the country. His driving himself through all weather to preach in the country made him so sick he nearly died, especially weakening his throat to repeated infection for the rest of his life. In both New York and Philadelphia his insistence on discipline offended several members, including some wealthy ones. Pilmoor arrived in Philadelphia May 14, 1772, and found Asbury preaching. Said Pilmoor,

> But O what a change. When I was here before the great Church would hardly hold the congregation; now it is not near full! Such is the fatal consequence of contending about *opinions* and the ministering of *discipline*. It grieves me to the heart to see the people scattered that we have taken such pains to gather; but I cannot help it without opposing the measures of Mr. Wesleys delegate, and that would breed much confusion, so I am obliged to go weeping away.[7]

Some other events are more difficult to relate to Asbury. Pilmoor made a remarkable missionary tour to the south, from May 8, 1772, to June of 1773:

> As we have now got preachers to take care of the people that God has graciously raised up by us in New York and Philadelphia and all the adjacent places, Mr. Boardman and I have agreed to go forth in the name of the Lord, and preach the gospel in the waste places of the wilderness and seek after those who have no shepherd.[8]

It is not clear whether Asbury was influential in his going. On his return to Philadelphia, Pilmoor flatly states, "Mr. Boardman and I had been shamefully misrepresented to Mr. Wesley," but he makes no specific charge that Asbury did the misrepresenting.[9] Asbury had been complaining about the operation of the American

[7] Pilmoor, Journal, pp. 154-55.
[8] April 30, 1772; Pilmoor, Journal, p. 150.
[9] July 13, 1773, Pilmoor, Journal, p. 266.

preachers ever since his arrival.[10] On October 10, 1772, he had received a letter from Wesley commending strict Methodist discipline and naming him Wesley's "assistant" for America, succeeding Boardman.

Asbury was not prepared to give unity to American Methodism as soon as he was put in charge. Wesley himself would hardly have been able to do that. However, he accelerated the sampling of the circuits and the touring of the whole connection which was to make him the best known, best informed, most indispensable Methodist in America. He left New York strengthened by his new status from Wesley and hoping the New York society would be obedient and strict in their Methodism from this time forth. He went to Philadelphia, where Boardman had gone, and conferred with him about his new position. Things looked pretty peaceful in Philadelphia: "All things considered, the people here seemed to be quiet and in good order." [11] Now was the time to get acquainted with the Methodists in Maryland. So he went south after the manner of traveling Methodist preachers—preaching some mornings at five, preaching some afternoons, preaching most evenings, preaching two or three times on Sunday, holding family prayers and worship at many stops, visiting prisoners, attending and preaching funerals when invited, riding twenty to fifty miles per day on horseback.

Methodism in the south looked good to Asbury. There was a "weakness of the instruments"—Strawbridge and his young lay preachers were rough, emotional, and untrained. There were "some little irregularities"—Strawbridge was administering the sacraments though he was not ordained. But there was revival here too: "The Lord hath done great things for these people, notwithstanding the weakness of the instruments, and some little irregularities." [12] There were crowds to hear preaching. Careless men became new men. Vigorous young fellows joined the ranks of the preach-

[10] November 19 and 21, 1771; January 1, 1772; December 7, 1772; JLFA, I, 10, 16, 57.
[11] October 26, 1772; JLFA, I, 48.
[12] November 5, 1772; JLFA, I, 50.

ers. The societies multiplied. It may be that Asbury already had an inkling that the giant strength of Methodism was to come from the south. The following summer Maryland would be reporting 500 Methodist members when New York had 180, Philadelphia 180, Virginia 100, and New Jersey 200.

In Asbury's *Journal* we have the earliest record of a quarterly meeting. This was a regional meeting of the southern preachers to arrange their stations and agree on procedures. In these earliest days such a meeting was basic to Methodist organization. The quarterly meeting convened on December 22, 1772, at Joseph Presbury's in Maryland. Asbury preached on Acts 20:28 "Take heed, therefore, unto yourselves"; he includes his sermon outline. Then the following propositions were raised:

1. What are our collections? We found them sufficient to defray our expenses.
2. How are the preachers stationed? Brother Strawbridge and brother Owings in Frederick county. Brother King, brother Webster, and Isaac Rollins, on the other side of the bay; and myself in Baltimore.
3. Shall we be strict in our society meetings, and not admit strangers? Agreed.
4. Shall we drop preaching in the day-time through the week? Not agreed to.
5. Will the people be contented without our administering the sacrament? John King was neuter; brother Strawbridge pleaded much for the ordinances; and so did the people, who appeared to be much biased by him. I told them I would not agree to it at that time, and insisted on our abiding by our rules. But Mr. Boardman had given them their way at the quarterly meeting held here before, and I was obliged to connive at some things for the sake of peace.
6. Shall we make collections weekly, to pay the preachers' board and expenses? This was not agreed to. We then inquired into the moral characters of the preachers and exhorters. Only one exhorter was found any way doubtful, and we have great hopes of him. Brother Strawbridge received £8 quarterage; brother King

and myself £6 each. Great love subsisted among us in this meeting, and we parted in peace.[13]

Asbury worked happily in Maryland and Delaware into the
spring of 1773. His typical circuit at Baltimore was one of two
hundred miles with twenty-four appointments, which he covered
every three weeks. Meanwhile he was receiving disquieting reports
from the north. Pilmoor, who had previously complained against
Wesley and Boardman, now extended his grumbling to Asbury.
In December, Asbury said he "received a letter from Mr. Pilmoor
which surpassed everything I ever had met with from a Methodist
preacher." [14] In February he had letters from both New York and
Philadelphia. "They entreat me to return, and inform me that
trouble is at hand." Back in Philadelphia in April, he was hammer-
ing away at Methodist discipline: "dealing closely" with the members in society, preaching on "stony-ground hearers," and deplor-
ing religion which is of no value but only "cumbereth the
ground." Before he got to New York to strengthen discipline there,
he was relieved as Wesley's assistant and another man was put in
charge.

Captain Thomas Webb may have been the agent of the change.
He coveted the best of Methodist leadership for America. On a
trip to England in 1772, Webb visited Wesley and the conference
of Methodist preachers in session at Leeds. Webb wanted John
Wesley to come to America or to send some ordained Anglican
clergy who would serve the Methodists. Failing that, he made
his plea that some of England's strongest and most mature Methodist men be sent so that the work in America might be stable.
Wesley sent two of his very best, Thomas Rankin and George
Shadford. Rankin had been a successful traveling preacher and
colleague of Wesley in England for nearly twelve years. He was the
new Wesleyan assistant for America, succeeding Asbury.

Not a ripple of discontent marred the new arrangement at its
beginning. Asbury was a youngster of twenty-seven years and of

[13] December 23, 1772; JLFA, I, 59-60.
[14] December 7, 1772; JLFA, I, 57.

limited experience. He himself had been hoping Wesley would come over to shape and direct the work in America personally. Now Wesley could not come, but he was sending a supervisor more mature than Asbury. Shadford, whom Wesley prized, was to be a new colleague. Wesley's letter to Shadford just before his sailing is a gem.

> Dear George—The time is arrived for you to embark for America. You must go down to Bristol, where you will meet Thomas Rankin, Captain Webb and his wife.
>
> I let you loose, George, on the great continent of America. Publish your message in the open face of the sun, and do all the good you can.—I am, dear George,
>
> > Yours affectionately.
> > John Wesley[15]

Asbury seems to have been completely candid when he entered in his *Journal* for June 3, 1773: "To my great comfort arrived Mr. Rankin, Mr. Shadford, Mr. Yearby, and Capt. Webb." [16]

The good relationship soon went sour. Rankin was not a very winsome preacher but he was stout for regular Methodist discipline. In the month after his arrival he called the preachers together for a conference in Philadelphia. Asbury records the results

> Our general conference began: in which the following propositions were agreed to:—
> 1. The old Methodist doctrine and discipline shall be enforced and maintained amongst all our societies in America.
> 2. Any preacher who acts otherwise, cannot be retained amongst us as a fellow-labourer in the vineyard.
> 3. No preacher in our connexion shall be permitted to administer the ordinances at this time; except Mr. Strawbridge, and he under the particular direction of the assistant.
> 4. No person shall be admitted, more than once or twice, to our love feasts or society meetings, without becoming a member.

[15] LJW, VI, 23.
[16] JLFA, I, 80.

5. No preacher shall be permitted to reprint our books, without the approbation of Mr. Wesley, and the consent of his brethren. And that Robert Williams shall be allowed to sell what he has, but reprint no more.

6. Every assistant is to send an account of the work of God in his circuit, to the general assistant.

There were some debates amongst the preachers in this conference, relative to the conduct of some who had manifested a desire to abide in the cities and live like gentlemen. Three years out of four have been already spent in the 'cities. It was also found that money had been wasted, improper leaders appointed, and many of our rules broken.[17]

It was not Rankin's zeal for discipline and itinerancy which gave offense to Asbury. He was a champion of both of these and may have been sparking the "debates" to which he refers. Evidently Rankin had a heavy-handed manner which made it hard for him to bear the freer style of the Americans and enlist their support. Asbury became a recognized center of resistance to him. His *Journal* is full of grumblings against Rankin. An acid test came at the conference of preachers in May of 1774. Asbury took a substantial part in the arguments in conference and had his way over Rankin. But when the conference was over, Asbury had been stationed at New York. New York was not where he wanted to be; he had wanted very much to go back to the revivals and the new Lovely Lane meeting house of Baltimore circuit. Under Boardman's earlier administration Asbury had declared, "I have not yet the thing which I seek—a circulation of preachers, to avoid partiality and popularity. However, I am fixed to the Methodist plan, and do what I do faithfully as to God." [18] Now, under Rankin's administration, he did not seem able to bear his own restriction.

When Rankin moved him to Philadelphia, according to plan, things only got worse. Asbury did not want to be in Philadelphia, and since Rankin himself was there the two irritated each other constantly. Asbury was sick to the point of death at both New

[17] July 14, 1773; JLFA, I, 85.
[18] November 19, 1771; JLFA, I, 10.

York and Philadelphia, but whenever he had strength he complained about Rankin and gathered support for his plan to return to Baltimore. Each was bidding for supporters among the Methodists of America; each was writing to Wesley stating his side of the case. It was a kind of blessed relief when they both left Philadelphia in February of 1775, Asbury returning to his beloved Baltimore. It is not clear whether he ever had Rankin's official permission to go.[19]

Rankin was a man of mediocre gifts but great zeal who was charged with unifying and purifying American Methodism. Francis Asbury was a much younger man who knew America and Americans better than Rankin did. When Rankin moved awkwardly and made mistakes, Asbury would cry that he was ruining the work. So Asbury was a threat to Rankin. Also, Rankin was a Tory who felt that the revolution of the Americans was a signal for all good Englishmen to return home. Asbury, though an Englishman, intended to stay. Rankin wanted Wesley to pull Asbury out of the American colonies, and evidently Wesley sent half-hearted instructions for his removal. But he sent them to Rankin, and Rankin never faced Asbury with them. The relation was eased in 1775 when Rankin first announced that he would return to England. It was eased further in 1778 when Rankin actually sailed for home. Nevertheless, Asbury always felt that Rankin had deliberately poisoned Wesley's mind against him and against the American Methodists.[20] It was an offense hard to forgive.

---

[19] John J. Tigert, A Constitutional History of American Episcopal Methodism (Nashville: Publishing House of the M.E. Church, South, 1916), pp. 75-81.

[20] To Joseph Benson, January 15, 1816; JLFA, III, 546-47. Cf. Albea Godbold, "Francis Asbury and His Difficulties with John Wesley and Thomas Rankin," Methodist History, April, 1965, pp. 3-19; Jesse Hamby Barton, "The Definition of the Episcopal Office in American Methodism" (Unpublished dissertation, Drew University, 1960), pp. 27-32.

3
DURING THE WAR

Francis Asbury did not choose to give much thought to the revolt of the American colonies from England. Years later he phrased it "Methodist preachers politicians! What a curse!" [1] Bunker Hill, Boston, Long Island, Trenton, Philadelphia, Valley Forge, Monmouth merited no notice in his *Journal* as they became newsworthy during the war. On the Declaration of Independence and the treaty with France he has no word. Political revolution was not essentially his business; in fact, he seems to have viewed this war as an unfortunate interruption of his primary concern, the extension of Methodism. When the people were keyed up about tea riots, British raids, and military musters, they were too heated to attend to preaching properly.

Imagine Asbury's dismay when John Wesley chose to take sides in the revolution. Wesley began this early. First he sided with the protesting colonists in his *Free Thoughts* in 1768; convinced that the colonists had a point in their protest against oppression, he wrote Lord North and the Earl of Dartmouth in June of 1775 to

[1] Jacob S. Payton, "Preachers in Politics," *Methodist History,* July, 1963, p. 15.

tell them so. But later that year he read Samuel Johnson's *Taxation No Tyranny* and found it completely convincing. Johnson's tract took a clear stand on the side of the English government and was violently opposed to the colonies. Wesley abridged it slightly and issued it as his own *Calm Address to Our American Colonies*. Wesley's edition outsold Johnson's swimmingly—forty thousand copies sold in twenty days. Johnson was appreciative; Tories on both sides of the ocean were delighted; American friends and patriots were infuriated. Wesley produced five more pamphlets bearing directly or indirectly on the revolution. Asbury said: "I . . . am truly sorry that the venerable man ever dipped into the politics of America." [2]

Some other Methodist preachers dipped into the politics of the revolt. Captain Webb spoke against the revolution. Martin Rodda distributed British propaganda labeling the revolting colonists as traitors; Rodda was associated in the public mind with Chauncey Clowe, organizer of an armed Royalist group in Delaware. All the Methodist missionaries from Great Britain were put through much searching of heart. They wanted to stay and they wanted to go. Asbury and Shadford, for example, agreed to spend a day together in fasting and praying to seek guidance about what they should do. After the prayer Asbury felt he should stay in America; Shadford felt he must return to England. Asbury concluded that one of them must be wrong, but Shadford believed that was not necessarily true. Perhaps it was God's will that Shadford go and Asbury stay.[3] That was the way things worked out.

Eight official Methodist missionaries had been sent from England to America in the years 1769-74: Pilmoor and Boardman in 1769, Asbury and Wright in 1771, Rankin and Shadford in 1773, Dempster and Rodda in 1774. As the revolt took shape, all returned to England except Asbury and Dempster. Rankin wrote Asbury in August of 1775 that he and Rodda and Dempster had concluded they should leave for England. Asbury's response was:

[2] March 19, 1776; JLFA, I, 181.
[3] *The Lives of Early Methodist Preachers, Chiefly Written by Themselves*, ed. Thomas Jackson (6 vols. London: Wesleyan Conference Office, 1865), VI, 172-73.

I can by no means agree to leave such a field for gathering souls to
Christ, as we have in America. It would be an eternal dishonour to
the Methodists, that we should all leave three thousand souls, who
desire to commit themselves to our care; neither is it the part of a
good shepherd to leave his flock in time of danger: therefore, I am
determined, by the grace of God, not to leave them, let the consequence be what it may.[4]

When the last of the missionaries sailed in 1778 Asbury was still
of the same mind.

Because of their British connections, even the Methodist preachers born in America were suspect during the war years. They had
been raised from among their peers in the American classes and
trained on the colonial scene. They were essentially as American
as could be. However, some patriots thought all Methodist preachers were British agents; some opponents of the Methodists were
glad to label them as Tories so they could abuse them freely. So
John Littlejohn barely escaped the tar and feathers in summer of
1775. William Watters was violently charged as a Tory by an
Anglican parson! Freeborn Garrettson, a conscientious objector to
participation in warfare, was treated to beating and imprisonment;
he narrowly missed hanging on two occasions. Philip Gatch was
painfully injured in incidents involving tarring and arm twisting.
Joseph Hartley refused to take the state oaths of Maryland and
Virginia; when they jailed him in Maryland he did his preaching
from the prison window. Jesse Lee was drafted for the North
Carolina militia. When the combined arguments of commissioned
and noncommissioned officers were not enough to convince Lee to
bear arms, the colonel assigned him to drive the baggage wagon for
the Methodist cook. Besides serving the country as a teamster, Lee
preached to the troops.[5]

Asbury heard of the preachers' hardships and used his influence

---

[4] August 7, 1775; JLFA, I, 161.

[5] William Warren Sweet, *Virginia Methodism* (Richmond: Whittet and Shepperson,
1955), pp. 75-91; John McLean, *Sketch of Rev. Philip Gatch* (Cincinnati: Swormstedt
and Poe, 1854), pp. 45-48; Leroy M. Lee, *The Life and Times of the Rev. Jesse Lee*
(Louisville: John Early, 1848), pp. 87-91.

to help the sufferers when he could. His influence was spotty at best. If this was the way American Methodist preachers were treated, what could he expect as an English preacher with the mark of the Tory Wesley upon him? Maryland began screening out undesirable preachers by enforcing an old license law; Asbury was fined ten pounds. Then in 1778 he found he must take the Maryland oath if he would work in that colony. Every male over eighteen must affirm:

> I, A.B., do swear that I do not hold myself bound to yield any allegiance or obedience to the King of Great Britain, His heirs or successors. And that I will be true and faithful to the State of Maryland, and will to the utmost of my power, support, maintain, and defend the freedom of independence thereof and the Government as now established against all open enemies and secret and traitorous conspiracies, and will use my uttermost endeavours to disclose and make known to the Government or some one of the judges or justices thereof, all treasons, or traitors, conspiracies, attempts or combinations against this State, or the Government thereof which may come to my knowledge. So help me God.[6]

Asbury was not ready to take this strenuous oath. He was still a British subject. As a preacher he did not choose to bear arms.

In Delaware the oath was less stringent and preachers were not required to take it. Early in 1778 Asbury moved to Delaware. He later said he could have taken the Delaware oath with a clear conscience and would have done it except that he did not want to hurt the tender consciences of others.[7] His host in Delaware was Judge Thomas White of Kent County. It is difficult to see why he chose to stay with White. As a staunch Anglican and a non-participant in the revolution, White was already under suspicion of the colonial authorities. Perhaps it took that kind of man to invite Asbury under the circumstances. On April 2, 1778, Judge White was arrested for interrogation. Asbury fled to new hiding

---

[6] HAM, I, 165 (quoted from the manuscript Journal of John Littlejohn).
[7] April 11, 1778; JLFA, I, 267.

places until April 29, and then returned to White's. This was to be his residence until April of 1780.

For the first few months he lived very quietly at his refuge in Delaware. He did not want to endanger Judge White or himself. Few things are more awful to contemplate than a caged Methodist itinerant, especially Francis Asbury. The Sundays he could not preach he called "dumb silent Sabbaths," and he hated them cordially. He crammed these days with hour upon hour of study. Never had there been so much time for his books before. He read Flavell, Hartley, Alleine, Doddridge, Bunyan, Barclay, Hervey, Prideaux, Hinde, Fletcher, Edwards, Sherlock, Comber, Salmon, Rutherford, and some books on medicine. He even read the Presbyterian Westminster Standards, including confession, catechism, form of government, and directory for worship: "Now I understand it better than I like it." [8] More than these he read Wesley, especially Wesley's *Notes upon the New Testament*. Most of all he read the Bible, over and over, in three languages. For a while it was his custom to read only the book of Revelation and Wesley's notes on that book on Sunday. So the *Journal* notation for May 10, 1778: "On the Lord's day I read the Revelation three times over, experienced great sweetness in my soul, both in reading and family exercises." [9] It was Asbury's insight that "the devil will let us read always if we will not pray," so in the midst of his studies he scheduled hour upon hour of prayer. All this afforded him neither peace nor satisfaction. He worried and anguished and was "assaulted by Satan" until the reader of the *Journal* wonders how long the poor refugee can last.

When help came, it came in the form of work. Asbury began preaching at Judge White's house, and at Judge White's barn, and at Edward White's house, and at Edward White's barn, and among the neighbors. He ventured out farther into the vicinity. Before long there was a circuit. "I laid a plan for myself to travel and preach nine days in two weeks. This was one step towards my former regularity in what appears to me as my duty, my element,

[8] November 17, 1779; JLFA, I, 323.
[9] JLFA, I, 270.

and my delight." [10] Now that he was a circuit rider, he met with the other preachers at quarterly meeting. Occasionally he was invited to ride some distance to preach. Best of all, the preachers of the larger connection did not forget him. Freeborn Garrettson came to visit. Preachers exchanged letters with him; already he was becoming a sort of symbol and information clearing center for American Methodism. By the spring of 1780 he was a recognized citizen of Delaware. Governor Rodney had given him a passport and had written letters to influential men on his behalf. The colonial military authorities had read some of Asbury's letters and knew his sympathy with the Americans. It was safe to ride out again.

The two years in Delaware were not a lost period in exile. Asbury made it plain later that a lot of work had been going on; Methodist membership in the peninsula increased by 1,800 while he was there. But it is easy to sense the excitement in his *Journal* as he returns to the great circuit of the whole connection in 1780:

I have been very much exercised in mind; the time for leaving this place draws nigh. Never was confinement in one State, Delaware, so trying to me.[11]

I am in peace, and much blest always when travelling.[12]

I was never more devoted to God—it makes me think I am in my duty. I was tempted and tried in Delaware to prepare me for, and drive me to, this work; and believe if I had not started I should have suffered great loss in my soul. I admire the hand of God in disposing of me, and wonder and own his providence.[13]

I have travelled so much that it seems like confinement to rest one day; I hope I shall travel as long as I live; travelling is my health, life, and all, for soul and body.[14]

[10] July 18, 1778; JLFA, I, 276.
[11] March 29, 1780; JLFA, I, 342.
[12] June 17, 1780; JLFA, I, 357.
[13] August 4, 1780; JLFA, I, 371.
[14] October 12, 1780; JLFA, I, 383.

Within this six months, I have travelled, according to my computa-
tion, two thousand six hundred and seventy-one miles; yet am uneasy
when still.[15]

One of the main reasons Francis Asbury found his confinement
to Delaware so hard to endure was his worry about the welfare of
the whole Methodist connection in America. Not that oversight of
the American Methodists had been officially committed to him.
When Rankin left the colonies, control of the connection was to
reside in a committee. The conference of 1777 named William
Watters, Philip Gatch, Daniel Ruff, Edward Dromgoole, and William Glendenning to the committee. Asbury was not mentioned at
all in connection with the committee. In fact, the official Minutes
for 1777 name Asbury as one of the fourteen assistants for that year
but indicate no station for him. Manuscript Minutes prepared by
Philip Gatch and by William Duke indicate that Asbury was
stationed at Annapolis.[16] Rankin would have prepared the Minutes;
it seems fruitless to speculate whether Rankin assumed Asbury
would take over as assistant and so left him without specific assignment, or whether Rankin wanted Asbury out of the American
picture and so did not care to mention him at all.

Whatever Rankin thought, Asbury was the Methodist of greatest stature and of warmest Wesleyan connection in America. His
mind was at work on ways to preserve at least a splinter of "old
Methodism" in Delaware if not a whole Wesleyan connection
throughout the colonies. There was nothing automatic about his
leadership. He was honored by the preachers in the middle colonies,
but in the south the connection was growing nicely without him
and was not anxious to be reminded of its European heritage. If he
was to lead, he would have to assert leadership.

Asbury's major challengers were the native southern preachers

[15] November 7, 1780; JLFA, I, 387.
[16] *Minutes of the Methodist Conferences Annually Held in America, from 1773 to
1794* (Philadelphia: Printed by Henry Tuckniss, sold by John Dickins, 1795), pp. 20-
21; Philip Gatch, Minutes . . . 1777; William Duke, Minutes . . . 1777; photostats of
Gatch and Duke Minutes at The Methodist Publishing House, Nashville.

who wanted Methodists to administer the sacraments. They had never been very closely bound to English Wesleyanism. They had the example of Strawbridge, who had administered the sacraments from the beginning, though unordained. They worked in Anglican colonies where the established clergy were not of a type they wanted their people to hear; exceptions like Devereux Jarratt and Charles Pettigrew were not enough to reverse the feeling that Anglicans were too worldly to deserve Methodist allegiance. Now, in the war years, there were even fewer Anglican clergy available to serve their own people or the Methodists. The fascination of the time was with things independent and American rather than with things formally correct and English. Remarkably, none of the younger men who entered the ministry under Strawbridge had imitated his sacramental practice. But the time for this was at hand. At the conference at Deer Creek in 1777 some American preachers wanted separation from the Church of England and the right to administer the sacraments. The decision was to take no step that year to separate. It was evidently an action to wait and see. At the Leesburg conference of 1778 the issue was once more held over to the next conference, in spite of protests. The drift was plain. The situation of colonies, people, and preachers in the south conspired to produce an independent Methodist church.

Asbury had begun to take leadership while he was in Delaware. He met with his friends from the northern stations at Judge White's home on April 28, 1779. This was twenty days before the regularly scheduled conference in Fluvanna County, Virginia. This Delaware caucus was conducted exactly like a conference, a preliminary session for the convenience of northern preachers and for the safety of Asbury and Ruff, who dared not travel to Virginia. Among those present were Asbury, Ruff, Watters, Garrettson, Caleb Pedicord, and William Gill. They voted to avoid separation from the Church of England, to endorse Asbury as Wesley's official assistant with full powers in America, and to send Watters to represent their views at the coming conference at Fluvanna. Asbury wrote in his *Journal*:

Our conference for the northern stations began at Thomas White's.
All our preachers on these stations were present, and united. We had
much prayer, love, and harmony; and we all agreed to walk by the
same rule, and to mind the same thing. As we had great reason to
fear that our brethren to the southward were in danger of separating
from us, we wrote them a soft, healing epistle. On these northern
stations we have now about seventeen travelling preachers.[17]

Constitutionally this was "an irregular Conference composed
of a small minority of preachers . . . unexpectedly, if not illegally,
convened." [18] Nevertheless, it was a very astute move. Asbury now
had a recognized position as assistant when the southern brethren
did not have a candidate. And he had the solid nucleus of a constituency which gave him a basis for negotiation. On May 3, 1779,
he wrote letters to four leading preachers in the south urging them
to avoid any action which would lead to an open break. His pleas
were not immediately heard; one wonders if he expected that they
would be. The conference at Fluvanna County met at Broken Back
Church and put the matter of Methodist sacraments to a vote.
Eighteen preachers, a majority, voted to change the rules to allow
Methodists to administer them. A polity was adopted to give
method to the action. Philip Gatch, Reuben Ellis, James Foster,
and Leroy Cole were constituted a presbytery to ordain each other
and then to ordain as many of the preachers as wished to administer the sacraments to Methodists.[19] If this was defeat for Asbury,
it was only defeat in the first skirmish. The major battle lay ahead.

On April 25 of 1780, Asbury was back in conference session
with his northern preachers. He was no longer confined to Delaware and presided over this meeting in Baltimore, though he was
not allowed to preach in Maryland. The southern brethren sent
Philip Gatch and Reuben Ellis to represent them. Now began a
most dramatic series of negotiations. Asbury's northern preachers
condemned the southerners for their presbytery and sacraments
and renounced them as no Methodists. They set up terms of

[17] April 28, 1779; JLFA, I, 300.
[18] Tigert, *Constitutional History*, p. 98.
[19] Gatch, Minutes . . . 1779.

return so hard that Gatch and Ellis would not even agree to take them to the southern conference. Then Asbury thought "to propose a suspension of the ordinances for one year, and so cancel all our grievances, and be one." [20] Gatch and Ellis finally agreed to return to the southern session at Manakintown on May 9 with this proposal. Asbury, Watters, and Garrettson went along as a peace delegation from the north. Such fighting, preaching, praying, and weeping: "O! what I felt!—nor I alone!—but the agents on both sides! they wept like children, but kept their opinions." [21] It looked like union was lost when almost miraculously the southerners agreed to suspend their sacraments for a year. They would write to Wesley for his opinion and convene a joint session of northerners and southerners at Baltimore in 1781 so the question could be more fully resolved. Meanwhile, Asbury was requested "to ride through the different circuits and superintend the work at large." [22]

Such was the task to which Asbury set himself when he came out of his semi-exile in Delaware in 1780. He must visit every possible society and regularize it according to old Methodist standards. He must marshal his northern forces so that no ground would be lost. He must win over the southern people and their preachers. He must fill the circuits with preachers and plan new circuits. He worked especially hard in Virginia and North Carolina, where the opposition centered. At the conference at Baltimore in 1781 Wesley's word was plain: continue on the old plan until further direction. Thirty-nine preachers voted to support Asbury and Wesley; Asbury said there was one opponent, though his vote is not recorded in the Minutes. Asbury presided and stationed the preachers. Six months later the war came to an end at Yorktown. Asbury was confronted with opportunity unlimited. From this time on he was *de facto* superintendent of the American Methodists.

[20] April 25, 1780; JLFA, I, 347.
[21] May 9, 1780; JLFA, I, 350.
[22] William Watters, *A Short Account of the Christian Experience and Ministereal Labours of William Watters* (Alexandria, Va.: S. Snowden, 1806), p. 81.

4
TOWARD A NEW CHURCH

When the revolution was ended in 1783, John Wesley could take a new look at his Methodist societies in America. They had grown! The numbers about tripled between 1776 and 1783, the very years of the war. Where there had been 24 preachers, 12 circuits, and 4,921 members there were now 82 preachers, 39 circuits, and 13,740 members.[1] That growth had not come so much in New York and Philadelphia. Those two cities had suffered attack and occupation by the British army; New York had actually decreased in membership. It was the Maryland, Delaware, Virginia, and North Carolina Methodists who had added the great numbers. These were the Anglican colonies, where faithful Anglican clergymen were few and the people were in fact unchurched. These were southern colonies, where the revivals came; after sharing in the Virginia revival with Devereux Jarratt just prior to 1777, the Methodists added circuits until almost half their American membership was in Jarratt's territory. In 1783, 89 percent of Methodist membership was below what would be the Mason-Dixon line. From

[1] *Minutes of the Annual Conferences of the Methodist Episcopal Church, 1773-1828* (New York: Mason and Lane, 1840), pp. 7, 17-18.

these southern revivals came the young preachers to man the circuits which would fill the great spaces of the south and west. Their churchly tradition was not strong. They were a long way from Wesley.

Wesley held a high view of the sacrament of the Lord's Supper. He practiced frequent Communion himself and he wanted all Methodists to be faithful communicants in the Church of England. The societies in America had no real chance to hold that standard. Not many Church of England clergy remained in the colonies. Of those who remained, only a few were willing to meet with the Methodists—William Stringer in Philadelphia, Samuel Magaw in Delaware, Jarratt in Virginia, Pettigrew in North Carolina, Uzal Ogden in New Jersey. But how could such a handful of clergy administer sacraments to all the Methodists besides doing the work of their own parishes? Many American Methodists had not partaken of the Lord's Supper in years, and their children were largely unbaptized.

Francis Asbury viewed the matter practically and spoke very little about sacraments in his preaching before 1784.

> We have joined with us at this time, those that have been Presbyterians, Dutch, and English, Lutherans, Mennonites, low Dutch and Baptists. If we preach up ordinances to these people, we should add, "if they are to be had, and if not, there can be no guilt." If we do any other way, we shall drive them back to their old churches.[2]

A substantial group of Methodist lay preachers felt themselves called both to preach and to administer the sacraments. They were restive until freed to do both. Wesley was going to have to resolve the matter and do it soon. Should he lower Methodist standards to a mere occasional Communion of some Methodists with some Anglicans? Or should he attempt to get Anglican clergy sent to America specifically to serve the Methodists? Or should he ask the Anglicans to ordain some Methodists? Or should he encourage those Methodists who wanted to administer the sacraments themselves?

[2] To John Wesley, September 20, 1783; JLFA, III, 31.

Then there was the matter of superintending the Methodists in America. Francis Asbury was making continuous rounds of the work: New York to New Jersey to eastern Pennsylvania, Delaware, Maryland, Virginia, and then into the back country to the newer settlements of Virginia and North Carolina. He was ordering the societies and doing his best to keep the southern preachers in line with "old Methodism." He had not been given an official title, but it was plain that he was the man best acquainted with the field. Wesley had letters from Asbury's friends in America who did not wish to have him removed or superseded. Asbury's own letters indicated that he wanted to stay.

> No person can manage the lay preachers here so well, it is thought, as one that has been at the raising of the most of them. No man can make a proper change upon paper, to send one here, and another [sic] without knowing the circuits and the gifts of all the preachers, unless he is always out among them. . . . I have laboured and suffered much to keep the people and preachers together: and if I am thought worthy to keep my place, I should be willing to labour and suffer till death for peace and union.[3]

Wesley sent Asbury a letter on October 3, 1783, just a month after the peace was signed. It was a letter intended for all American preachers, but it must have been especially sweet to Asbury's ears.

> Let all of you be determined to abide by the Methodist doctrine and discipline published in the four volumes of *Sermons* and the *Notes upon the New Testament,* together with the *Large Minutes* of the Conference. . . .
> I do not wish our American brethren to receive any who make any difficulty of receiving Francis Asbury as the General Assistant.[4]

This gave American Methodism a temporarily clear status. It was to be like English Methodism in belief and structure. And it was to be under the direction of Wesley's man, Francis Asbury.

[3] *Ibid.,* pp. 31-32.
[4] LJW, VII, 191.

The American preachers, including Asbury, must have known that Wesley could not simply let the matter rest there. However, Asbury was not pressing for further revision. There is some evidence that he would have settled for the *status quo* with himself as supervisor of the Methodists in the New World and with the sacraments left in oblivion at least for a time. It is hard to unify his expressed thoughts about the sacraments.

> I see clearly that to press the people to holiness, is the proper method to take them from contending for ordinances, or any less consequential things.[5]

> I have laboured to get our friends well affected to the Episcopal Church; what could I do better, when we had not the ordinances among us? [6]

> I reverence the ordinances of God; and attend them when I have opportunity; but I clearly see they have been made the tools of division and separation for these three last centuries. . . . If young men of our connection should get ordained, it will not do well.[7]

Perhaps he still hoped that Wesley would come to America, or that some Anglican clergy who were also Methodists could be sent from Wesley, or that there could be some merger of the Methodists with a reinvigorated Anglicanism in the new nation.

However much Wesley may have depended on his general assistant, there is no indication that he consulted Asbury directly about a new plan for forming a Methodist Church in America. Wesley had tried in 1780 to get Bishop Robert Lowth of London to ordain a Methodist. Bishop Lowth maintained that the Methodist lacked education. Wesley replied on August 10 that the church would do better to ordain this experienced and pious Methodist preacher than many Anglican clergy already sent to America who knew a little Greek and Latin but knew no more how to save souls than how to catch whales.[8] Such recriminations did little for

[5] May 18, 1780; JLFA, I, 351.
[6] May 23, 1780; JLFA, I, 353.
[7] September 20, 1783; JLFA, III, 31.
[8] LJW, VII, 31.

the scattered Methodist societies of America. Wesley could neither expect that the Anglicans would ordain enough men to help the Methodists nor hope that such ordained men would be put under Methodist direction.

Wesley had a trusted associate named Thomas Coke, an Oxford-trained civil lawyer and a Methodist with all the zeal of a convert. In February of 1784 Wesley called Dr. Coke into his private room in London and outlined his new plan for establishing a Methodist Church in America complete with ordained clergy. Further, he suggested that Coke be the one to go to America to ordain the Methodist preachers. Coke, like Wesley, was both a Methodist preacher and an ordained minister or presbyter of the Church of England. Wesley was quite sure from his studies that presbyters, being of essentially the same order as bishops, had the power to ordain, and further, to ordain a bishop from their own number.

The plan was simple, clear, and shocking to almost all Anglicans. Charles Wesley expressed his feeling in a rhyme.

> So easily are Bishops made
> By man's, or woman's whim?
> Wesley his hands on Coke hath laid,
> But who laid hands on Him? [9]

Coke was convinced of the rightness of the action but wanted as much support from Wesley as he could muster. He wanted Wesley himself to ordain him as bishop and to ordain Whatcoat and Vasey as the presbyters who were to accompany him.

So on September 1, 1784, at Bristol, Wesley ordained Richard Whatcoat and Thomas Vasey deacons. These were the first Methodist ordinations. Wesley wrote in his *Journal* for that day: "Being now clear in my own mind, I took a step which I had long weighed in my mind." [10] Next morning Wesley ordained Whatcoat and Vasey presbyters or elders, the next higher order of clergy, and

[9] *Representative Verse of Charles Wesley,* ed. Frank Baker (Nashville: Abingdon Press, 1962), p. 368.
[10] *The Journal of the Rev. John Wesley,* ed. Nehemiah Curnock (London: Epworth Press, 1938), VII, 15.

Thomas Coke as "superintendent." The way was now clear for Methodists to ordain Methodists in the New World.

When Coke, Whatcoat, and Vasey sailed from Bristol on September 18, 1784, they carried at least five documents to the American brethren. Three were the ordination certificates for Coke, Whatcoat, and Vasey—all signed by John Wesley. The fourth was a letter from Wesley to "Our Brethren in America." It is one of the most basic documents of American Methodism.

1. By a very uncommon train of providences many of the Provinces of North America are totally disjoined from their Mother Country and erected into independent States. The English Government has no authority over them, either civil or ecclesiastical, any more than over the States of Holland. A civil authority is exercised over them, partly by the Congress, partly by the Provincial Assemblies. But no one either exercises or claims any ecclesiastical authority at all. In this peculiar situation some thousands of the inhabitants of these States desire my advice; and in compliance with their desire I have drawn up a little sketch.

2. Lord King's *Account of the Primitive Church* convinced me many years ago that bishops and presbyters are the same order, and consequently have the same right to ordain. For many years I have been importuned from time to time to exercise this right by ordaining part of our travelling preachers. But I have still refused, not only for peace' sake, but because I was determined as little as possible to violate the established order of the National Church to which I belonged.

3. But the case is widely different between England and North America. Here there are bishops who have a legal jurisdiction: in America there are none, neither any parish ministers. So that for some hundred miles together there is none either to baptize or to administer the Lord's supper. Here, therefore, my scruples are at an end; and I conceive myself at full liberty, as I violate no order and invade no man's right by appointing and sending labourers into the harvest.

4. I have accordingly appointed Dr. Coke and Mr. Francis Asbury to be Joint Superintendents over our brethren in North America; as also Richard Whatcoat and Thomas Vasey to act as elders among

them, by baptizing and administering the Lord's Supper. And I have prepared a Liturgy little differing from that of the Church of England (I think, the best constituted National Church in the world), which I advise all the travelling preachers to use on the Lord's Day in all the congregations, reading the Litany only on Wednesdays and Fridays and praying extempore on all other days. I also advise the elders to administer the Supper of the Lord on every Lord's Day.

5. If any one will point out a more rational and scriptural way of feeding and guiding those poor sheep in the wilderness, I will gladly embrace it. At present I cannot see any better method than that I have taken.

6. It has, indeed, been proposed to desire the English bishops to ordain part of our preachers for America. But to this I object; (1) I desired the Bishop of London to ordain only one, but could not prevail. (2) If they consented, we know the slowness of their proceedings; but the matter admits of no delay. (3) If they would ordain them now, they would likewise expect to govern them. And how grievously would this entangle us! (4) As our American brethren are now totally disentangled both from the State and from the English hierarchy, we dare not entangle them again either with the one or the other. They are now at full liberty simply to follow the Scriptures and the Primitive Church. And we judge it best that they should stand fast in that liberty wherewith God has so strangely made them free.[11]

The fifth document was *The Sunday Service of the Methodists in North America*. Wesley believed in dignity and order and stability in the services of the church. This was his book of liturgy and services. It contained orders for morning and evening prayer; a litany; readings and prayers for the Christian Year; the ritual for the sacraments and for ordination of deacons, elders, and superintendents; selected Psalms; and Wesley's abridgment of the Thirty-nine Articles of the Church of England.

Coke, Whatcoat, and Vasey arrived in New York on November 3, 1784. In America the Methodists were no longer to be simply a connection; they were to be a church.

Asbury knew the men from England were coming. He must

have expected some news of considerable importance. He was going his appointed rounds of the circuits, quarterly meetings, and conferences.

> There seems to be some call for me in every part of the work: I have travelled at this time from north to south to keep peace and union: and O! if a rent and separation had taken place, what work, what hurt to thousands of souls! [12]

> I have reason to bless God who hath made me, and doth make me, a center of union among preachers, and the people; and that he hath given me the hearts of both so much.[13]

Since the conference of 1783 at Baltimore he had traveled a fantastic route, extending from New York to a winter visit to the raw new settlements in the back country of Virginia and North Carolina.[14] At the conference at Baltimore on May 25, 1784, he had silenced the opposition of William Glendenning and some other rebels by reading his commission as general assistant. "Mr. Wesley's letter settled the point, and all was happy." [15] He had the scars and the spurs of a general assistant who knew the men and the circuits of the whole vast enterprise which was the American Methodist connection. He was the best known and best informed Methodist in America, and he knew it.

Dr. Coke and Richard Whatcoat came to Barratt's Chapel in Delaware on the weekend of November 14, 1784. They had been preaching in New York, and at St. Paul's Anglican Church in Philadelphia, and at the commodious home of Richard Bassett at Dover. Francis Asbury also approached Barratt's Chapel, from the south, to take part in the quarterly meeting with his preachers of that region. They were to enjoy a revival meeting, resolve the problems of their circuits, and take their new assignments in as much peace as possible. Asbury was late enough for church on Sunday that he did not get to converse with Coke or Whatcoat

---

[12] May 17, 1780; JLFA, I, 351.
[13] To his parents, June 7, 1784; JLFA, III, 37.
[14] See map, JLFA, I, 457.
[15] JLFA, I, 460.

before service. In the Communion service he was surprised to see that Whatcoat assisted; Asbury had known him as an unordained preacher back in England. They all had Sunday dinner, along with eleven preachers, at the Barratt home nearby, and then Coke took Asbury aside in private to explain the whole new plan. Asbury reacted like an Englishman: "I was shocked when first informed of the intention of these my brethren in coming to this country: it may be of God." [16]

However, Asbury was also an American who had learned some lessons in his rounds. If the new plan was to work, the American preachers must be involved in it from the start, and a substantial majority must approve it all the way. A word from Wesley was not enough. Americans did not take well to any direction from England; the authority must reside in the body of the preachers themselves. So he said he would accept Wesley's appointment to serve along with Coke as superintendent only if the preachers chose him. He began by putting the matter up for discussion before the preachers who were immediately present at the quarterly meeting. They thought a thing of this importance called for a special meeting of all the Methodist preachers in the land. It was this council of preachers who promptly called such a conference to be held at Christmas at Baltimore. Coke had feared from the start that Asbury might lay some roadblock in the way of the new plan. So when Asbury moved forward with the plan, Coke conquered his own shock and surprise at such democratic tactics and did it Asbury's way. Asbury's way was to get the program he wanted through the actions of the American preachers. He was too wise to try to impose a program upon freedom-intoxicated circuit riders directly.

Preparations must now be made for the Christmas Conference, just over one month away. Freeborn Garrettson was sent to get the word to all the preachers in time for them to attend. Garrettson rode more than twelve hundred miles within six weeks, but he was a Methodist itinerant at heart so he stopped to preach once or twice a day as he went. Some complained that he went too slowly and

[16] November 14, 1784; JLFA, I, 471.

depended too much on the mail; Jesse Lee in Virginia did not get word of the conference until December 12, and he counted such loitering as without excuse.[17] Asbury wanted Coke to get a look at the Americans: "I was very desirous the Doctor should go upon the track I had just been over, which he accordingly did." [18] This meant a horseback ride of nine hundred miles or so for Coke, accompanied by popular "Black Harry" Hosier, the first Negro Methodist preacher in America. Asbury also arranged preaching tours for Whatcoat and Vasey; he himself managed to meet Coke on December 14 at Abingdon in Maryland to talk about founding a school there. During the week before Christmas, Asbury, Coke, Whatcoat, Vasey, and William Black were among those who met at Henry Gough's house near Baltimore to set up the agenda and shape the proposals for the conference.

The crucial Christmas Conference began its meeting on December 24, 1784. The stewards had put backs on the benches in Lovely Lane Meeting House and had installed a stove. Coke presided, preached the opening sermon, presented the letter from Wesley to "Our Brethren in America," and made a further verbal statement of Wesley's intentions. Every part of the new plan was adopted. The conference was in session ten days; Coke preached every day at noon and was a key figure in the ordaining of deacons and elders. Coke's name was even placed first in the title chosen for the new Cokesbury College which Coke and Asbury were to plan.

But if Coke was first in protocol, Asbury was still the prominent man. He actually knew the American church; he had the confidence and affection of a large body of the preachers. Asbury's candid account of the conference embodies the text of his ordination certificate.

Continued at Perry Hall until Friday, the twenty-fourth. We then rode to Baltimore, where we met a few preachers: it was agreed to form ourselves into an Episcopal Church, and to have superintendents, elders, and deacons. When the conference was seated, Dr. Coke

[17] Jesse Lee, *A Short History of the Methodists in the United States of America* (Baltimore: Magill and Clime, 1810), p. 89; Leroy Lee, *Life of Jesse Lee*, p. 129.

[18] November 14, 1784; JLFA, I, 472.

and myself were unanimously elected to the superintendency of the Church, and my ordination followed, after being previously ordained deacon and elder, as by the following certificate may be seen.

Know all men by these presents, That I, Thomas Coke, Doctor of Civil Law; late of Jesus College, in the University of Oxford, Presbyter of the Church of England, and Superintendent of the Methodist Episcopal Church in America; under the protection of Almighty God, and with a single eye to his glory; by the imposition of my hands, and prayer, (being assisted by two ordained elders,) did on the twenty-fifth day of this month, December, set apart Francis Asbury for the office of a deacon in the aforesaid Methodist Episcopal Church. And also on the twenty-sixth day of the said month, did by the imposition of my hands, and prayer, (being assisted by the said elders,) set apart the said Francis Asbury for the office of elder in the said Methodist Episcopal Church. And on this twenty-seventh day of the said month, being the day of the date hereof, have, by the imposition of my hands, and prayer, (being assisted by the said elders,) set apart the said Francis Asbury for the office of a superintendent in the said Methodist Episcopal Church, a man whom I judge to be well qualified for that great work. And I do hereby recommend him to all whom it may concern, as a fit person to preside over the flock of Christ. In testimony whereof I have hereunto set my hand and seal this twenty-seventh day of December, in the year of our Lord 1784. THOMAS COKE.

Twelve elders were elected, and solemnly set apart to serve our societies in the United States, one for Antigua, and two for Nova Scotia. We spent the whole week in conference, debating freely, and determining all things by a majority of votes. The Doctor preached every day at noon, and some one of the other preachers morning and evening. We were in great haste, and did much business in a little time.[19]

Thus Wesley's assistant, Francis Asbury, who would not administer the sacraments on his recent tour because he was not ordained by a bishop was now a bishop empowered to ordain others. He whose position had been tenuously based on the fact that he was on

[19] December 18, 1784; JLFA, I, 474-76.

the scene, supported by some knowledge of the field and some acceptance by the people, was now superintendent with a book of discipline for America and a book of worship for America in his hands. The new order was approved by both Wesley and the preachers themselves. Norman Spellmann's point is clear and convincing that Wesley intended to ordain a bishop and call him a superintendent. Wesley's later protest against the use of the title "bishop" in America was meant to rebuke Asbury for pride and especially for failing to take Wesley's vocabulary. But Wesley ordained to an office of bishop; both he and his contemporaries understood that.[20] The Methodists had launched an independent and national organization for America. For as long as he could keep the body of his preachers disciplined, Francis Asbury was to be the man to test the new church in operation.

[20] Norman Spellmann, "The Formation of the Methodist Episcopal Church," HAM, I, 201-6.

5
TIME OF TESTING

As soon as the Christmas Conference was over, Francis Asbury got back on the road. Fifty miles through a snowstorm was the first day's ride. A new type of entry began to appear in the *Journal:*

> We read prayers, preached, ordained brother Willis deacon, and baptized some children. . . . Preached and administered the sacrament.[1]

> Nothing could have better pleased our old Church folks than the late step we have taken in administering the ordinances; to the *catholic* Presbyterians it also gives satisfaction; but the Baptists are discontented.[2]

Generally the people were glad to be a Methodist Episcopal Church with clergy instead of a connection of religious societies. That much about the action had been clear: it formed a Methodist Epis-

[1] January 9 and 15, 1785; JLFA, I, 480.
[2] January 28, 1785; JLFA, I, 481.

copal Church under the direction of superintendents, elders, deacons, and helpers.

Some things about the new church had been easy to adopt on the basis of common tradition. There was Wesley's revision of the English *Book of Common Prayer,* now renamed *The Sunday Service.*[3] This book of ritual included Wesley's purged version of the English Thirty-nine Articles as a doctrinal statement. Wesley's abridgment had twenty-four articles carefully screened to exclude Romanism, high-church ritualism, and Calvinism, to which the American Methodist fathers added one more article recognizing the powers of the new government of the United States.[4] There was also the revision of the English Methodist Large Minutes done by Coke, Asbury, and others; this was to embody the essential rules of the new church and be the backbone of the *Discipline.*[5] Some further proposals had been easily agreed to out of common conviction. For example, the superintendent was to be ordained only after consent of a majority of the conference. The superintendent was to preside at conferences; assign the preachers to circuits; receive, change, or suspend preachers as necessary; and receive appeals for decision from both preachers and people.

But there were a great many facets of the new church about which little or nothing was said. What was to be the term of office and the orderly method of succession for superintendents and for elders? What was the precise delineation of the office of elder? How was the membership of the conference to be made up in a constituency expanded too far to hold frequent central meetings of all traveling preachers? Was every conference to be absolutely free to change any principle of the church's government by a simple majority vote? How were the decisions of the superintendent to be related to the decisions of the conference?

These were questions to be resolved in the experience of the su-

[3] See Nolan B. Harmon, "The Book of Common Prayer and the American Churches," *Religion in Life,* XVIII (1949), 508-22.

[4] See Nolan B. Harmon and John W. Bardsley, "John Wesley and the Articles of Religion," *Religion in Life,* XXII (1953), 280-91.

[5] See Tigert, *Constitutional History,* pp. 208, 532-602.

perintendents as they carried on their work. Who were the superintendents who would actually do this? On the lists of the new
church there were three: John Wesley, Thomas Coke, and Francis
Asbury. John Wesley was now an old man who was never coming
to America again. Thomas Coke was not very well accepted by the
American preachers. One said of him:

> At first, I was not at all pleased with his appearance. His stature,
> complexion, and voice, resembled those of a woman rather than those
> of a man; and his manners were too courtly for me. So unlike was
> he to the grave, and, as I conceived, apostolic Mr. Asbury, that his
> appearance did not prepossess me favourably. He had several appoint-
> ments in the circuit, to which I conducted him; and, before we
> parted, I saw so many things to admire in him that I no longer
> marvelled at his being selected by Mr. Wesley to serve us in the
> capacity of a superintendent.[6]

In any case, Coke stayed in America less than six months after the
Christmas Conference. After a tour in the north, a trip with Asbury to visit George Washington, and a brief appearance at the
conference of 1785, he sailed back to England on June 2. Coke
often returned to America, coming nine times between 1784 and
1803 and crossing the Atlantic eighteen times in all. These were
fleeting visits rather than solid episcopal tours. So the crucial work
of testing the new church in operation fell on Francis Asbury.

Asbury had some ideas of his own about the way the new church
should be run. He felt that the office of superintendent was precisely that of a bishop. Wesley and Coke had renewed the primitive line of bishops of the early church, long corrupted and lost.
He, Francis Asbury, was now the most valid bishop in America.
He began at once to wear the gown and garb of a bishop of the
Church of England for Sunday services. When some of his frontier
preachers poked fun at this[7] he gave up the garb rather than make
an issue of it. But he did not give up his view of the bishop's office

[6] Thomas Ware, *Sketches of the Life and Travels of Rev. Thomas Ware* (New York:
Mason and Lane, 1839), p. 108.
[7] Leroy Lee, *Life of Jesse Lee*, p. 149.

and power. To be sure, it was the conference of preachers who elected him bishop and he was amenable to their action as a body. But until and unless they acted to remove or discipline him, he was the leader of the whole church, preachers and people. Asbury never subscribed to the theory that the bishop and the preachers were equal. A bishop is chosen to rule. The Christmas Conference had elected Asbury bishop. He intended to rule as long as he held the office. Of course he would do the bidding of the conference, but as bishop he expected that in most cases he himself would shape what the bidding of the conference would be.

The conduct of the conferences was in his favor. Typically it was Asbury who formulated and presented the questions for discussion. The items he presented made the agenda of the meeting. He was the one who knew best which were the sharpest issues and chief concerns of the church. So he posed each issue in a pointed or even loaded question for discussion. In effect, most of the motions would be made by Asbury. He spoke to the motions as he was inclined, and he presided over the whole discussion. Soon he learned how to lose a vote with some grace. He knew the difference between the important and the less important. On the less important matters he demonstrated his grace; on the more important matters he managed to prevail.

It was not practical to have all the preachers meet at one place for conference each year. This would take them from their work in the circuits for too many weeks and leave the people exposed to the predatory tactics of "John's people," the Baptists. Besides, there was the precedent of having the conference in two sessions, dating back to Asbury's practice of convening the northern preachers separately in 1779.

This was the way business was handled in the new church. In a typical case, Asbury would formulate a question and take it through three sessions of a conference in the same year. The brethren in Carolina, South or North, would have their say. Then the Virginians would vote in their session. Baltimore settled the matter in the final session. If the question passed all three sessions, or even Baltimore and one other, it had been decided by the conference. Remember that Asbury typically phrased the question, presented it to each session, spoke to the issue, presided, and kept the minutes. Preachers were examined, received, dismissed, or assigned to circuits at all the conference sessions without further reference. In fact, Asbury could do this personally at any time in his role as bishop. If Superintendent Coke happened to be in America, Asbury loaded him generously with preaching and presiding duties. He kept the handling of business firmly in his own hands.

For some reason, Wesley never quite understood the system. Perhaps this was because he never understood the hyperdemocratic drive and pushiness of the American frontiersman. In England, Wesley might consult his preachers, but he himself then did the deciding and the decision was final. His rulings were to be kept and not amended. In America, as Asbury knew, the preachers must both discuss and decide. A bishop must know how to work through this procedure. A letter from Wesley to Asbury on October 31, 1784, indicates that Wesley had some feeling for the precarious stance of the American Methodist administrator:

> You are aware of the danger on either hand: and I scarce know which is the greater? One or the other, so far as it takes place will overturn Methodism from the foundation: Either our travelling Preachers turning Independents, & gathering Congregations each for himself: Or procuring Ordination in a regular way, & accepting Parochial Cures. If you can find means of guarding against both evils the work of God will prosper more than ever.[8]

Nevertheless, he seems not to have grasped the radical nature of American democratic bias. Whether or not a thing was democratic, it had to look democratic.

The crisis came in 1786. The American Methodists had laid their regular plans for three sessions of the conference in 1787. There was to be one in North Carolina in May, one in Virginia in June, and one in Maryland in July. The schedules of all horse-

[8] First published in HAM, I, 211.

back preachers were attuned to this plan, bishop and circuit riders alike. Then on September 6, 1786, Wesley wrote to Coke that he should call a general conference for America to meet in May at Baltimore. Probably, for Wesley, this seemed like a considerable concession to democracy and the American plan! He went on to direct that the American preachers should elect Richard Whatcoat to be a new superintendent for the American Methodists with Asbury. It was also his plan to name Freeborn Garrettson superintendent for Nova Scotia.[9]

Coke was accustomed to the Wesleyan way of doing things and simply wrote the Americans a letter from overseas giving proper instructions. The American preachers gathered in Baltimore on May 1, but they were in a poor mood for work. Their schedules had been upset. Freeborn Garrettson did not want to go to Nova Scotia permanently. Several were opposed to the election of Whatcoat as superintendent and were afraid that his election might compromise Asbury's leadership. Asbury had written Whatcoat, "The mode of appointment is not approved of, though many of us by no means object to the person."[10]

Coke had come over from England to preside. When he felt the displeasure of the assembly he reminded them of their pledge in 1784 to obey Wesley's commands so long as he lived. Under the circumstances this reminder was a mistake. A majority voted to rescind that pledge to be obedient to Wesley and to remove Wesley's name from the American Minutes. Further, on the second day of the conference, Coke prepared and signed a certificate:

> I do solemnly engage by this instrument, that I never will, by virtue of my office, as superintendent of the Methodist church, during my absence from the United States of America, exercise any government whatever in the said Methodist church during my absence from the United States. And I do also engage, that I will exercise no privilege in the said church when present in the United States, except that of ordaining according to the regulations and

[9] LJW, VII, 339; HAM, I, 426-27.
[10] March 25, 1787; JLFA, III, 49.

law, already existing or hereafter to be made in the said church, and
that of presiding when present in conference, and lastly that of travelling at large. Given under my hand the second day of May in the
year 1787.[11]

Asbury was, as usual, the kingpin of the conference, but he did
not leap to the defense of Wesley or of Coke. At the time he said
in his *Journal,* "We had some warm and close debates in conference; but all ended in love and peace." [12] Later he said he was mute
when the minute of obedience to Wesley was adopted in 1784 and
he was mute when it was expunged in 1787.[13] He would have been
the one who actually omitted Wesley's name from the Minutes.
And in that 1787 edition of the General Minutes appeared the word
"bishop" for the first time. Wesley's word "superintendent" was
going out and Asbury's usage of "bishop" was coming in.

Wesley was never fully reconciled. The conference of 1787,
after refusing his direction, wrote him a "long and loving" letter
suggesting that he come to America to visit. In 1789 Wesley's
name was re-entered in the American Minutes as a courtesy, though
it was plain that only Coke and Asbury had been elected to actually superintend. Wesley was not mollified. The depth of the old
man's feeling came out in the last letter which Asbury received
from him. It came on March 15, 1789; Asbury called it "a *bitter
pill* from one of my greatest friends." [14]

There is, indeed, a wide difference between the relation wherein
you stand to the Americans and the relation wherein I stand to all
the Methodists. You are the elder brother of the American Methodists: I am under God the father of the whole family. Therefore
I naturally care for you all in a manner no other persons can do.
Therefore I in a measure provide for you all; for the supplies which
Dr. Coke provides for you, he could not provide were it not for me,
were it not that I not only permit him to collect but also support
him in so doing.

[11] Lee, *Short History,* p. 122.
[12] May, 1787; JLFA, I, 538.
[13] November 28, 1796; JLFA, II, 106.
[14] JLFA, I, 594.

But in one point, my dear brother, I am a little afraid both the Doctor and you differ from me. I study to be little: you study to be great. I creep; you strut along. I found a school: you a college! nay, and call it after your own names! O beware, do not seek to be something! Let me be nothing, and "Christ be all in all!"

One instance of this, of your greatness, has given me great concern. How can you, how dare you suffer yourself to be called Bishop? I shudder, I start at the very thought! Men may call me a knave or a fool, a rascal, a scoundrel, and I am content; but they shall never by my consent call me Bishop! For my sake, for God's sake, for Christ's sake put a full end to this! Let the Presbyterians do what they please, but let the Methodists know their calling better.

Thus, my dear Franky, I have told you all that is in my heart. And let this, when I am no more seen, bear witness how sincerely I am Your affectionate friend and brother,

John Wesley[15]

After that conference in May of 1787, the Methodist Episcopal Church did not return to the old pattern of two or three sessions of one conference, hinged and completed at Baltimore for each year. From now on Baltimore was not so much the center of the church. The church, in fact, seemed to have no center. The number of sessions in the annual conference multiplied. There were six sessions of the 1788 conference, eleven of the 1789 conference, fourteen of the 1790 conference, and seventeen of the 1792 conference. And there was Francis Asbury, carrying his questions from one session to the next, trying to get positive action from each on every piece of legislation. Small wonder that he worked out what he considered an improvement in the system.

In 1789 he took his new idea to each of the eleven sessions of the conference for approval. The idea was that much of the church's business should be carried on by a "council" composed of the bishops and certain presiding elders, always a body of at least nine. Asbury hoped this would be a small and efficient group which could meet anywhere and anytime on the call of the bishop. Since the

[15] September 20, 1788; LJW, VIII, 91; cf. HAM, I, 424-28.

members would be appointed by the bishop, and presumably removed by the bishop, he evidently hoped there would always be unity in the ranks so that unanimous approval of the council could be required for any action. Incidentally, this would give him a veto on any proposition. Since Asbury expected the same good acceptance which he received as he took his questions from session to session in the conference, he made the further democratic proposal that no action of the council would bind any region until a majority of their session of the conference approved. It was a plan which combined a kind of simplicity with continued control by Asbury. The preachers would continue to speak and vote on every issue; the business would be done by a small, efficient, and obedient group. There would be no need for an expensive and inconvenient general conference of all the preachers—which Asbury did not want anyway.

The proposed council was approved, it was established, and it met twice.[16] Asbury may actually have felt it was going to work, as soon as some amendments were made and the noise of some critics died down. But instead of peace there came a thirty years' war over the power of the episcopate. Not many were sensitive about the nullification which might result if some conference sessions refused to endorse council actions. But a great many were sensitive about the absolutism which might result from the bishop's control of the council's personnel. Preachers were uneasy about being even one step removed from the process of decision making; they had a feeling of being left out, and the more irate claimed that Asbury was putting them completely out of active church government.

Some giants among the preachers were opposed to the council. Jesse Lee, Thomas Coke, and James O'Kelly favored a plan for a periodic general conference of the whole church to act in the interests of the whole church. Asbury was always uneasy at the thought

---

[16] *Proceedings of the Bishop and Presiding Elders of the Methodist-Episcopal Church in Council Assembled* (Baltimore: Goddard and Angell, 1789); Lee, *Short History*, pp. 149-56.

of such a series of general conferences, any one of which gave opportunity for a phalanx of dissident preachers to upset the whole church government, and even Asbury himself. But he knew when he was whipped; the opponents would not be downed. O'Kelly not only opposed the council; he deliberately organized opposition to the appointive power of the episcopacy and especially to Asbury as the wielder of it. Lee would not be silenced by a curt letter from the council advising him to quit his protest or leave the church.[17] Coke arrived in America early in 1791 and pressed for a general conference, especially in view of O'Kelly's hue and cry. Said Asbury: "I felt perfectly calm and acceded to a general conference, for the sake of peace." [18]

The first Methodist General Conference met on Thursday, November 1, 1792, at Baltimore with Thomas Coke presiding. Since a fight was expected, there was a large representation. Asbury did not even want to hear the word "council"; he was ready to let the council die in peace if only he could get this conference finished without more trouble. He tried to get the business preworked by a "preparatory committee, to keep order and bring forward the business with regularity," a kind of remnant of the function of the council. This failed because the preachers wanted to debate everything fully anyway.

O'Kelly was not to be satisfied just because the council was abandoned and this General Conference called. He wanted now to use the conference for his more basic project, whittling down the power of Bishop Asbury. Early on the second day, Friday, O'Kelly made his motion: "After the bishop appoints the preachers at conference to their several circuits, if any one thinks himself injured by the appointment, he shall have liberty to appeal to the conference and state his objections; and if the conference approve his objections, the bishop shall appoint him to another circuit." [19] Everybody knew that Asbury was squarely opposed to any such

---

[17] Leroy Lee, *Life of Jesse Lee*, p. 270.
[18] February 23, 1791; JLFA, I, 668.
[19] Lee, *Short History*, p. 176.

action. It would subject the bishop to such harassment on the details of his appointments as to leave him neither peace nor power. When the "injured" preacher was relocated, what was to be done with the preacher thus displaced, and what would keep the displaced ones from appealing *ad infinitum?* The whole discussion was not compatible with Asbury's understanding of the role of the bishop.

Here was a subject close to every traveling preacher's heart. Everybody had an opinion. For two days the debate raged. There was a bit of cooling over Sunday, but all day Monday the arguments continued. Asbury chose to withdraw from the floor as soon as the motion was made. His own person and powers were involved in such a way that he preferred to have the matter resolved in his absence. Also he was sick, as usual. It appeared early in the discussion that the majority might support O'Kelly. The proposal looked democratic and O'Kelly had been enlisting support against the "tyranny" of Asbury for years. O'Kelly's rooms were now the strategy headquarters for the dissidents, and there were some excellent men among them. But somehow the bitter zeal of O'Kelly's forces backfired. Attacks on Asbury's power lacked taste when he was not there to hear or defend. Then too, Asbury played a master stroke; he killed his enemies with kindness. He sent this letter to the General Conference:

My Dear Brethren:—Let my absence give you no pain—Dr. Coke presides. I am happily excused from assisting to make laws by which myself am to be governed: I have only to obey and execute. I am happy in the consideration that I never stationed a preacher through enmity, or as a punishment. I have acted for the glory of God, the good of the people, and to promote the usefulness of the preachers. Are you sure that, if you please yourselves, the people will be as fully satisfied? They often say, "Let us have such a preacher;" and sometimes, "we will not have such a preacher—we will sooner pay him to stay at home." Perhaps I must say, "his appeal forced him upon you." I am one—ye are many. I am as willing to serve you as ever. I want not to sit in any man's way. I scorn to solicit votes.

•

I am a very trembling, poor creature to hear praise or dispraise. Speak your minds freely; but remember, you are only making laws for the present time. It may be, that as in some other things, so in this, a future day may give you further light. I am yours, &c.

Francis Asbury[20]

They took the vote at an extraordinary session on Monday night. O'Kelly's motion lost by a large majority.

Defeat was not bearable for O'Kelly. He was proud and ambitious as well as doggedly committed to democracy and primitive polity as he understood it. He could not submit. A conciliation committee found him unyielding. He and at least four of his followers picked up their saddlebags and walked out. Within a few months he formed his own Republican Methodist Church; within a year he had lured ten thousand Methodists into it, mostly in Virginia and the Carolinas. Asbury stated his appraisal of O'Kelly in his letter to Thomas Morrell a few days after the conference:

I believe now nothing short of being an episcopos was his first aim. His second was to make the Council independent of the Bishop and General Conference, if they would canonize his writings. This could not be done. His next step was with the authority of a pope to forbid me, by letter, to go a step farther with the Council, after carrying it once around the continent and through the first Council, which ordered me to go round and know the minds of the brethren. His following step was to write against me to Mr. Wesley, who he knew was disaffected to me, because I did not merely force the American Conference to accede to Mr. Wesley's appointment of Brother Whatcoat, which I did submit to Dr. Coke only for peace with our old *father*. How moved he then to make himself independent of me and the general connection, and dragged in the little Doctor, whom, a little before, he would have banished from the continent. Then he stipulated with me through the Doctor to let him stay in that station, and consented to leave the decision to a General Conference, and when the decision went against him, went away.[21]

[20] November 8, 1792; JLFA, I, 734.
[21] JLFA, III, 113.

A curious pamphlet war developed. O'Kelly wrote *The Author's Apology for Protesting Against the Methodist Episcopal Government,* an attack on episcopacy but more especially on the "popery" of Asbury. Nicholas Snethen championed Asbury and the Methodists in *A Reply to an Apology for Protesting Against the Methodist Episcopal Government.* O'Kelly opened round two with *A Vindication of the Author's Apology with Reflections on the Reply.* Snethen's rejoinder was *An Answer to James O'Kelly's Vindication of His Apology.* This sequence is symbolic of the fact that Asbury was never to see the end of this fight.[22] When he convinced the conference to award O'Kelly forty pounds a year as a sort of old-age pension, O'Kelly's followers cried "bribery." When he went to future sessions of the General Conference, ghosts of O'Kelly were always rising up to try to limit the episcopacy or make the office of presiding elder elective. O'Kelly himself lived on and kept the opposition alive. As late as 1805 the bishop made an entry in his *Journal* while in Virginia:

> Mr. O'Kelly has come down with great zeal, and preaches three hours at a time upon government, monarchy, and episcopacy; occasionally varying the subject by abuse of the Methodists, calling them aristocrats and Tories; a people who, if they had the power, would force the government at the sword's point. Poor man! [23]

Small wonder that when Asbury was old and his mind rambled it kept turning up bits and pieces of uneasiness and defense about O'Kelly.

However, 1792 had been the watershed. That General Conference decided that the church would remain episcopal and that Asbury would be bishop. It further established the place of the quadrennial General Conference at the very top of the growing institutional structure. Asbury seems always to have been ill at ease with the General Conferences because of their threat of instability.

---

[22] See Charles F. Kilgore, *The James O'Kelly Schism in the Methodist Episcopal Church* (Mexico City: Casa Unida De Publicaciones, 1963).

[23] February 13, 1805; JLFA, II, 459.

But they actually gave him bit by bit the stable polity he sought. The conference of 1796 regularized the nature and the territory of the annual conferences, now to be the centers of government and fellowship for the itinerants. The conference of 1808 established a principle of delegation for the make-up of its own membership and adopted restrictive rules so that basic doctrine or structure of the church could not be changed in any one year by a mere majority.

There was no lay representation in any of these conferences but Asbury was not sorry.[24] It was the traveling preacher who gave up all to serve. The traveling preacher and his traveling brothers had the interest of the church most at heart and should rule. And if anyone else wanted to share this right, let him become a traveling preacher!

---

[24] *The Doctrines and Discipline of the Methodist Episcopal Church in America. With Explanatory Notes, by Thomas Coke and Francis Asbury* (10th ed.; Philadelphia: Printed by Henry Tuckniss, sold by John Dickins, 1798), pp. 34-35.

PART II

The Bishop's Work

6
TRAVELER

Asbury's most significant episcopal action was simply to mount his horse and begin to be a bishop. He kept making the rounds until everybody knew him. In the south, where the churches were few and the ministers fewer, he gloried in the mushrooming growth of Methodist circuits. In the north, where non-Methodist congregations were well established and churches everywhere at hand, he sent ground-breaking preachers to win enough Methodists for him to visit. As he watched the settlers flow west along the Cumberland route he said, "We must take care to send preachers after these people." [1] Everywhere Asbury became the living symbol of Methodism. When Coke wanted to send Asbury a letter in 1787 he just addressed it "The Rev'd Bishop Asbury, North America." It was delivered.

This omnipresence of Asbury is a giant fact of American church history. The church establishments were just being broken. Most people were slow to realize what disestablishment would mean; Congregationalists did not recognize the facts for a full generation.

[1] October 14, 1803; JLFA, II, 410.

"Denomination" would be the new pattern. Francis Asbury was a denominational executive for church extension, a passionate denominationalist.

This task was very hard on the bishop's bones and flesh. Generally he traveled horseback. "I seldom mount my horse for a ride of less distance than twenty miles on ordinary occasions; and frequently have forty or fifty in moving from one circuit to another. In travelling thus I suffer much from hunger and cold." [2] Since another giant fact of American church history was the space of the western frontier, his national diocese kept expanding. Methodists who went west asked for Methodist preachers; Asbury sent Methodist preachers whether they were asked for or not. Soon his territory was about the size of continental Europe, excluding Russia, and he was still making the rounds himself. When he took time to add up his horseback mileage for a year, it generally totaled four to six thousand miles.

He literally went everywhere. In his annual or semi-annual episcopal journeys he visited practically every State in the Union every year. His Journal shows that he went into New York State more than fifty times; New Jersey, over sixty; Pennsylvania, seventy-eight; Maryland, eighty; North Carolina, sixty-three; South Carolina, forty-six; Virginia, eighty-four; Tennessee and Georgia, each twenty; Massachusetts, twenty-three times after his first visit there in 1791; and in the other States and Territories with corresponding frequency. Take an atlas and follow him on the map as he makes a typical journey [1791-92]. Leaving New York in the early part of September, he proceeds by Philadelphia, Wilmington, Baltimore; Alexandria, Petersburg, and Norfolk, Virginia; Raleigh, North Carolina; and Charleston, South Carolina, to Washington, in Georgia. Returning through South Carolina, he enters North Carolina; passes on to the western counties; crosses the mountains to the Holston River, in Tennessee; plunges into the Kentucky wilderness as far as Lexington; returns to the Holston; passes up on the west side of the Alleghenies, over a most mountainous region, through the whole breadth of Virginia, to Uniontown, in Pennsylvania;

[2] January 30, 1788; JLFA, I, 561.

crosses the Alleghenies by Laurel Hill and Cumberland to Baltimore; goes on to New York; proceeds directly through Connecticut
and Massachusetts to Lynn; passes west across the valley of the
Connecticut, by Northampton, and over the Berkshire Hills by Pitts-
field, to Albany, and then down the valley of the Hudson to New
York, where he arrives on the 28th of August, 1792. In later years
his episcopal circuit was even more extended.[3]

How can this be translated into aching days of travel by horse?
How does it feel to finish a western tour in Kentucky and know
that the next conference is in South Carolina only a few weeks
away? Those Appalachian Mountains, the Lord's dirtiest trick on
a horseback rider, lay there in the way. Asbury dreaded them; he
spoke of his forty times "over the Alps." The mountains were bad
enough when they were dry.

> I preached at Samuel Edney's. Next day we had to cope with
> Little and Great Hunger mountain. Now I know what Mills Gap is,
> between Buncombe and Rutherford: one of the descents is like the
> roof of a house, for nearly a mile: I rode, I walked, I sweated, I
> trembled, and my old knees failed: here are gullies, and rocks, and
> precipices; nevertheless, the way is as good as the path over the
> Table mountain—bad is the best.[4]

Usually the mountains were not dry. Consider the crossing in
March of 1797:

> I was unwell: the clouds were lowering. We had ridden but a
> mile when the rain began. . . . Hard necessity made us move for-
> ward: the western branch of Toe River, that comes down from the
> Yellow Mountain, was rapidly filling; and was rocky, rolling, and
> roaring like the sea, and we were compelled to cross it several times.
> When we came to ascend the mountain, we had a skirmish of rain,
> thunder, and lightning. . . . I found hard work to ride where Thomas
> White had driven his wagon, for which he deserves a place in my

[3] Ezra Squier Tipple, *Francis Asbury: The Prophet of the Long Road* (New York:
Methodist Book Concern, 1916), pp. 162-63.
[4] October 1, 1806; JLFA, II, 518.

journal and a premium from the State. When we had ascended the
summit of the mountain, we found it so rich and miry, that it was
with great difficulty we could ride along; but I was wrapped up in
heavy, wet garments, and unable to walk through weakness of body;
so we had it pitch, slide, and drive to the bottom. We then came
upon the drains and branches of Great Toe River. From Fisher's we
had to ride through what I called the *shades of death,* four miles to
Miller's. Here we had to cope with Toe River, and near the house
came into deep water. My horse drove to the opposite bank above the
landing, and locked one of his feet in a root, or something like it,
but freed himself. At last we made the house; the people received us
kindly, and gave us such things as they had. We could only par-
tially dry our garments. We heard heavy tidings of a deep rocky ford
yet to be passed in our way across Toe River.[5]

In June in West Virginia he remarked, "We have had rain for
eighteen days successively, and I have ridden about two hundred
miles in eight or nine days; a most trying time indeed." [6] Those
mountains were unforgettable. Asbury in Connecticut, searching
for adequate language for a terrible ten-mile stretch of road at
Stonington, "properly so called," muses, "I would almost as soon
undertake to drive over the Alleghany mountain." [7]

If the mountains were the bane of the west, the undrained land
was the bane of the south. Heading west meant "crossing the
Alps"; heading south meant "crossing the swamps." So in Virginia
in February of 1787, "Brother Poythress frightened me with the
idea of the Great Swamp, the east end of the Dismal; but I could
not consent to ride sixty miles round; so we ventured through,
and neither we nor our horses received any injury. Praise the
Lord! . . . I am now surrounded with waters and hideous swamps,
near the head of the Pasquotank River." [8] Then in North Carolina
he was traveling "three miles on the water, and . . . three more on

[5] March 24, 1797; JLFA, II, 124-25; JLFA reads "Doe River" at the end of this
entry.
[6] June 1, 1786; JLFA, I, 512.
[7] June 14, 1791; JLFA, I, 680.
[8] February 3, 1787; JLFA, I, 533.

roads under the water." [9] In South Carolina he was pathetically
thankful for a horse that swam so well: "I was not wet much
higher than my knees." [10] There are freighted words about "travelling through heavy rains, deep swamps in dark nights." Again
in February, near Charleston, "We came to the Cypress Swamp
in the night, following a poor Negro, who waded through as a
guide, and not expecting to find it as bad as it was: at length we
came to sister Browning's." [11]

So he wore out his horses, "Jane" and "Fox" and "Spark." Where
there was any semblance of a road he learned to travel in stout
but light carriages—which he would variously call a carriage,
chaise, sulky, or Jersey wagon. It is essential to remember that
most back country roads were little more than an indication of
direction, being for months at a time impassible oceans of mud.
The trick was learning how to veer off the road to the right or left
just far enough to find firm bottom to the mud within reach of the
horse but not far enough to get trapped or lost in the heavy timber.
Asbury took some pride in his skill as a bush driver.

> We set out for Crump's, over rocks, hills, creeks, and pathless
> woods and low land; and myself in the carriage. The young man with
> me was heartless before we had travelled a mile; but when he saw
> how I could bush it, and sometimes force my way through a thicket,
> and make the young saplings bend before me, and twist and turn
> out of the way, or path, for there was no proper road, he took
> courage; with great difficulty we came in about two o'clock, after
> travelling eight or nine hours; the people looking almost as wild as
> the deer in the woods; I preached on Titus ii, 10-12. [12]

Horses were always running away or falling from exhaustion or
going lame or otherwise obstructing the advance of the church.
It is not hard to imagine the fatigue points of that kind of travel.
As the bishop grew older, his diocese only widened in the raw new

[9] February 13, 1787; JLFA, I, 534.
[10] April 1, 1787; JLFA, I, 536.
[11] February 21, 1793; JLFA, I, 748.
[12] July 22, 1780; JLFA, I, 368.

west. "O, my jaws and teeth!" he wrote. On Friday the thir-
teenth of November in 1812 he rode forty-five miles through
Tennessee and lamented "O, the rocks, hills, ruts, and stumps!
My bones, my bones!" [13]

Asbury was his own doctor for his many ailments on the road.
He fancied himself knowledgeable in medicine, having done some
reading of the subject as Wesley had done. "Began this morning to
read books on the practice of physic: I want to help the bodies and
souls of men." [14] Asbury promoted the use and sale of John Wesley's *Primitive Physic*. Equally terrifying medical advice was
compiled in *The Family Adviser* by Dr. Henry Wilkins "at the
request of our friend Mr. Asbury." [15] These books were commended and sold through regular Methodist channels as an aid to
families "who have not the advantages of a physician."

Though he gave medical advice freely to all who would take it,
Asbury practiced primarily on himself. One catalog of his ailments says: "He suffered terribly from boils, fevers, inflammatory
rheumatism, sore throat, weak eyes, bronchitis, asthma, toothache,
ulcers in the throat and stomach, neuralgia, intestinal disorders,
swollen glands, skin diseases . . . , and finally galloping consumption." [16] Tartar emetic seems to have been his favorite remedy
and he took it frequently.[17] For ulcerated throat he used a gargle
of "sage tea, honey, vinegar, and mustard," and after that another
gargle of "sage tea, alum, rose leaves, and loaf sugar" to strengthen
the part.[18] During his severe illness in the summer of 1797 he
was actually stopped in his travels in New York, and here he con-
centrated on his medicine.

Finding myself swelling in the face, bowels, and feet, I applied leaves
of burdock and then a plaster of mustard, which drew a desperate

[13] JLFA, II, 631, 713.
[14] November 25, 1779; JLFA, I, 324.
[15] Henry Wilkins, *The Family Adviser* (5th ed.; New York: Hitt and Ware, 1814),
preface.
[16] Herbert Asbury, *A Methodist Saint: The Life of Bishop Asbury* (New York:
Alfred Knopf, 1927), p. 262.
[17] January 14, 1798; JLFA, II, 151.
[18] January 29, 1775; JLFA, I, 147.

blister. . . . I took cream of tartar and nitre daily, to cool and keep open the body. I also made use of the [cinchona] bark.[19]

Having survived to open the new year of 1798 in Virginia, he was regaining some strength and described his medical regimen.

I am now taking an extraordinary diet—drink made of one quart of hard cider, one hundred nails, a handful of black snakeroot, one handful of fennel seed, and one handful of wormwood, boiled from a quart to a pint, taking one wine glass full every morning for nine or ten days, using no butter, or milk, or meat; it will make the stomach very sick, and in a few days purge the patient well. I was better in my feelings than I have been since I have been taken ill.[20]

There seems to have been a great confidence in the medicinal benefits of raising strategic blisters with mustard plaster; one Kentucky doctor is said to have applied a plaster to his wife's head to draw out her Methodism, which he deplored.[21] Asbury seemed to have great faith in the technique: "A blister under my ear has removed the pain in my head." [22] But at times he applied the blisters with such abandon and thoroughness as to be crippling. However, it was a rare occasion when either his sicknesses or his treatments kept him from making the mileage appointed for the day.

Nor was his trouble always over when the day's ride was done. If he was on his regular round in the settled country, he might spend the night occasionally with wealthy Henry Gough or Governor Van Cortlandt or Senator Bassett or General Russell or Governor Tiffin. He learned that Widow Bond and Widow Bombry entertained him gladly; Mrs. Withey "kept one of the best houses of entertainment on the continent" and always "fed the Lord's prophets." [23] This kind of provision was rare enough in the settled country. For the six months of his annual tour on

[19] July 25, 1797; JLFA, II, 131.
[20] January 1, 1798; JLFA, II, 149.
[21] September 19, 1813; JLFA, II, 742-43.
[22] January 14, 1774; JLFA, I, 103.
[23] May 5, 1810, and June 7, 1800; JLFA, II, 636, 235.

the new frontier, comfort did not exist. There he slept in the barn lofts where he could see light through the roofs and sides in a hundred places. When he slept in a frontier cabin it was often "three deep"—three to any kind of bed.

> The people, it must be confessed, are amongst the kindest souls in the world. But kindness will not make a crowded log cabin, twelve feet by ten, agreeable: without are cold and rain; and within, six adults, and as many children, one of which is all motion; the dogs, too, must sometimes be admitted. On *Saturday*, at Felix Ernest's, I found that amongst my other trials, I had taken the itch; and considering the filthy houses and filthy beds I have met with, in coming from Kentucky Conference, it is perhaps strange that I have not caught it twenty times: I do not see that there is any security against it, but by sleeping in a brimstone shirt:—poor bishop! But we must bear it for the elect's sake. I wrote some letters to our local brethren, and read the book of Daniel while in this house.[24]

> O, how glad should I be of a plain, clean plank to lie on, as preferable to most of the beds; and where the beds are in a bad state, the floors are worse.[25]

> I have been obliged to sleep on the floor every night since I slept in the mountains. Yesterday I rode twenty-seven miles, and to-day thirty.[26]

> At night we were poorly provided against the weather; the house was unfinished; and to make matters worse, a horse kicked the door open, and I took a cold, and had the toothache, with a high fever.[27]

There were chiggers in the woods, fleas in the houses, and mosquitoes mingled with gnats in the air over both. There was no place to flee. The man Francis Asbury complained, "How few are there who would not choose strangling rather than life and the

[24] October 14, 1803; JLFA, II, 411.
[25] July 10, 1788; JLFA, I, 577.
[26] July 20, 1781; JLFA, I, 409.
[27] February 27, 1787; JLFA, I, 534.

labours we undergo, and the hardships and privations we are compelled to submit to! Blessed be God, we have hope beyond the grave!" [28] When one of his critics compared him to the pope, he said:

> For myself, I pity those who cannot distinguish between a pope of Rome, and an old, worn man of about sixty years, who has the *power given him* of riding five thousand miles a year, at a salary of eighty dollars, through summer's heat and winter's cold, travelling in all weather, preaching in all places; his best covering from rain often but a blanket; the surest sharpener of his wit, hunger—from fasts, voluntary and involuntary; his best fare, for six months of the twelve, coarse kindness; and his reward, suspicion, envy, and murmurings all the year round.[29]

But the bishop Francis Asbury always conquered the mere man Francis Asbury. He had to travel to do his work, and his work must be done. It was his custom to send no preacher into a territory which he did not himself visit. It is likely that no man knew America so well as he—the highways and byways of all the states and the actual settlements of people from Boston to Georgia or the Atlantic to Kentucky. One *Journal* entry says: "When we came to New Hope Creek we could not ford it; so I crossed on a log." [30] The very next entry is undaunted: "I am willing to travel and preach as long as I live; and I hope I shall not live long after I am unable to travel." [31] Perpetual motion was the mark of his ministry.

---

[28] July 8, 1782; JLFA, I, 428.
[29] December 15, 1803; JLFA, II, 417.
[30] March 12, 1782; JLFA, I, 422.
[31] March 17, 1782; JLFA, I, 422-23.

7

PREACHER

Everywhere he went, Francis Asbury preached. "I preached . . ." is his *Journal's* most typical entry. Preaching for the day sometimes began at 5:00 A.M. Wesley had preached at this early hour in England; Pilmoor had established the custom in the New World; Asbury followed the precedent of both. These early morning services were not simply family devotions. At New York the repeated entry was "many people" at five o'clock and "a moving time." [1]

The day also ended with preaching. Asbury said he looked forward to his pulpit in the evening, a sort of cordial before bedtime to insure his rest. The evening service would usually be appointed in advance. When the bishop's schedule was known, public notice of preaching would be given out for each place where he was to spend the night. Asbury was irritated if notice of his appointments was not properly given. Preaching was his lifework. The Word was a matter of life and death to the hearers. He did not want the arrangements for preaching sloppily made. But even if the announcement had not been properly given, the local Methodists

---

[1] See the entries for September 7–October 18, 1772; JLFA I, 42-47.

would gather a congregation on the spot when the bishop arrived, and Asbury would preach.

If the trip had been hard, or if the traveling party got lost on the trails, the bishop might arrive just in time for preaching without having had rest or food all day. This happened often enough to be discouraging but was no excuse to omit preaching. Rest and food could come when the congregation had gone home. The services were long. Asbury rarely preached less than an hour. But he seems never to have preached a predetermined sermon of a predetermined length. Rather, he preached to the particular congregation assembled. He tried to speak to their need; he responded to their response.

> I was much led out on Eph. vi, 18, and we were employed till nearly twelve o'clock at night.[2]

> Upon the whole I believe we were speaking about four hours, besides nearly two spent in prayer.[3]

> I preached at the chapel, to about four hundred serious people, from John iv, 48: I spoke for near two hours; perhaps it is the last time.[4]

If the people came in late, he continued all the longer.

> The people coming in still after I began, caused me to lengthen out my discourse.[5]

> I felt unwell, but went to the Point in the morning, where my mind was interrupted by the frequent coming of people, almost to the very end of the sermon. After the preaching was over, I told them that I had rather they would stay at home, than come in such an irregular manner.[6]

Between the morning preaching and the evening preaching there would be other opportunities. Some of these were appoint-

[2] March 28, 1788; JLFA, I, 565.
[3] January 22, 1790; JLFA, I, 622.
[4] November 14, 1779; JLFA, I, 322.
[5] November 1, 1787; JLFA, I, 553.
[6] November 24, 1776; JLFA, I, 205.

ments at regular preaching places honored by whatever Methodist preacher passed that way. Some were unforeseen chances to bear witness grasped at the moment they appeared. The family with whom Asbury spent the night could expect to be led in prayers, to be exhorted to Christian living, and to be examined, one by one, in their progress toward sanctification. The liveryman or the ferryman or the chance companion seeking shelter from the rain made congregation enough for Asbury. "A poor, unhappy man abused me much on the road: he cursed, swore, and threw stones at me. But I found it my duty to talk to him, and show him his danger." [7] He preached wherever his horse stopped! If he did not give all men the gospel, their blood might be on his hands. Extraordinary times demanded extraordinary means.

> The Lord hath enabled me, of late, to be faithful to the families which have come in my way. And we must overcome our natural bashfulness and backwardness, to assist the precious souls of our fellow-men, who are on the brink of endless ruin, and see it not. [8]

> I spent part of the week in visiting from house to house. I feel happy in speaking to all I find, whether parents, children, or servants; I see no other way; the common means will not do; Baxter, Wesley, and our Form of Discipline, say "Go into every house:" I would go farther, and say, go into every kitchen and shop; address all, aged and young, on the salvation of their souls. [9]

Nor was Sunday any day of rest for the bishop. Preaching at one point in the morning and at another in the vicinity in the evening was generally assumed. To this might be added an observance of the Lord's Supper and a love feast or a third preaching service. Asbury did not like to travel on Sunday except as this was absolutely necessary to reach a nearby preaching place. Because all the Methodist preachers were so hard at work on Sunday, Asbury became concerned about a day of rest for them. He came to urge that traveling preachers regularly take Monday as a day

[7] November 19, 1772; JLFA, I, 53.
[8] August 20, 1777; JLFA, I, 247.
[9] May 24, 1795; JLFA, II, 51.

to rest and study and write and pray. But he did not use Monday as a regular rest day for himself; any sort of rest day was very irregular with him.

Then there were special occasions which seemed to demand preaching. If there were Negro slaves bound to their plantation he would preach to them there. If there were soldiers at the barracks he would gather a crowd and preach. If the old folks were relegated to the poorhouse he would meet them there. If he could get the attention of the people at a dance hall or a tavern he preached there. If criminals were jailed he would visit them in their cells; if they were condemned he would attend their execution and harangue the crowd on the evanescence of life and the need for repentance.

Especially were there funerals. At least a hundred people attended most funerals, and as many as a thousand might attend. Here were people who might never be seen at a Methodist quarterly meeting, but they would come to a funeral and they would expect preaching there. Besides the prayers and reading of scripture at a funeral, there were usually a sermon, an exhortation, and a service at the grave. Asbury would take any of these parts if invited. Or he would do them all if needed. In one service by himself he said he spoke, service and exhortations in all, three hours.[10] When he spoke at the grave he sometimes gave a commentary on the burial service, presumably the one he read and used from the *Sunday Service* sent over by Wesley.[11]

Asbury wanted his sermons to be solemn, penetrating, and biblical. "Lord, keep me from all superfluity of dress, and from preaching empty stuff to please the ear, instead of changing the heart!" [12] Since he rarely wrote out any of his sermons, leaving extant only a few eulogistic remarks concerning some of his preachers, it is difficult to be certain what he preached. He did advocate good order in preaching and he did advocate preparation before speaking.

[10] January 24, 1780; JLFA, I, 332.
[11] January 26 and February 17, 1780; JLFA, I, 332, 336.
[12] May 29, 1774; JLFA, I, 116.

In preaching from Ephesians ii, 12, 13, I had great freedom. It seems strange, that sometimes, after much premeditation and devotion, I cannot express my thoughts with readiness and perspicuity; whereas at other times, proper sentences of Scripture and apt expressions occur without care or much thought. Surely this is of the Lord, to convince us that it is not by power or might, but by his Spirit the work must be done. Nevertheless, it is doubtless our duty to give ourselves to prayer and meditation, at the same time depending entirely on the grace of God, as if we had made no preparation.[13]

Asbury almost always took a biblical text for his preaching. Some 700 of his texts he noted in his *Journal*. He spoke of his texts fondly and respectfully in his daily record; it is likely that he spoke from them in the same way in his preaching. There are also some 175 sermon outlines recorded in the *Journal*. Only in a special sense can these outlines be said to be biblical. Asbury's most common practice was to take the wording of a biblical text and reconstruct from that wording a topical outline of his own for preaching. Where he knew the historical background of the text he might use it. If the text was obviously and directly applicable he might apply it literally. Finding a church fight in a New Jersey congregation, he used the text: "This is his commandment, that we should believe on the name of his Son Jesus Christ, and love one another." [14] But there was no guarantee that the topical outline drawn from a text would have any direct connection with the primary meaning of the text itself. So when Acts 20:28 said "Take heed . . ." Asbury came out with an interesting and very useful mixture of admonitions to watchfulness by preachers. Among other headings, they were to take heed to those under deep conviction, those groaning for full redemption, and those who had backslidden.[15] And if the text mentioned salvation, the topic headings would almost certainly cover the full range of crucial Methodist doctrines.

[13] August 1, 1774; JLFA, I, 126.
[14] I John 3:23; JLFA, I, 25.
[15] December 22, 1772; JLFA, I, 59.

Rode to Maxfield's, and preached to about three hundred people; spoke on "Lord, are there few that be saved?" First, showed, What we are to be saved from. 2. How we are saved. 3. Why there are few. No open sinner can be in state of salvation; no formalist, violent sectarian, having only opinions and modes of religion; no hypocrites or backsliders; no, nor those who are only seekers.[16]

The topics of the sermon tended to come out the same no matter what the text. There was (1) conviction—under awful weight of our sin; (2) repentance and justification—to be taken on now; (3) perseverance in good works—no backsliding; and (4) sanctification—going on to perfect love.

This making of texts into topics was the easier to do because of Asbury's free use of allegory; he warned his preachers against it but he used it himself. On a single page of the *Journal* he treated three Old Testament texts (Isa. 33:16; Isa. 62:6; and Song of Solomon 1:7), giving each phrase of all three a free and allegorical rendering into a topic for Methodist Christians.[17] And when he came to prophetic study of the book of Revelation he went ecstatic:

Was both instructed and delighted to-day in reading the Revelation with its comment. There we see the rise and spread of the Christian religion through the extensive and idolatrous empire of the Romans; the wars of the Saracens; the gradual rise and artful progress of Popery. What an amazing prophetic history is this, of all people and nations, in epitome! How expressive are the differently-coloured horses, and surprising representations seen by St. John! In this book, extraordinary events are foretold, as well as the proper rule of our faith and practice revealed. If this deep book were fully understood, need we go any farther after knowledge?

It seems rather strange that, till lately, I could discover no beauties in the Revelation of St. John. But now I think it is the grand key of all mysteries, whether pure or impure; opening to view all the revolutions, persecutions, and errors of the Church from that time

[16] November 22, 1779; JLFA, I, 323.
[17] May 24-27, 1773; JLFA, I, 79.

till the end of the world. And then it favours us with a glimpse of what shall remain forever.[18]

Asbury chose his text-topics to suit the stage of Christian life he wished to stress. If conviction of sin was what the people needed, he would introduce this topic with a terrifying text. There was the rich man and Lazarus of Luke 16 or the "piercing words of our Lord, 'Thou knowest not the day of thy visitation.' " [19] Or he might choose:

> Then whosoever heareth the sound of the trumpet, and taketh not warning; if the sword come, and take him away, his blood shall be upon his own head.[20]

> And it shall come to pass at that time, that I will search Jerusalem with candles, and punish the men that are settled on their lees: that say in their heart, the Lord will not do good, neither will he do evil.[21]

> Unto you first God, having raised up his Son Jesus, sent him to bless you, in turning away every one of you from his iniquities.[22]

> For the time is come that judgment must begin at the house of God: and if it first begin at us, what shall the end be of them that obey not the gospel of God? And if the righteous scarcely be saved, where shall the ungodly and the sinner appear? [23]

When awakening was the need, Asbury was an expert rouser in his intensely earnest way: "I was alarming, as the people appeared to me to be careless." [24]

When Asbury sought to lead his hearers out of the depths of sin, he had passages to point up his topic of repentance and justification. Such a text was "This is a faithful saying, and worthy of all

[18] April 23 and 29, 1774; JLFA, I, 113.
[19] Paraphrase Luke 19:44; JFLA, I, 149.
[20] Ezek. 33:4, September 29, 1772; JLFA, I, 45.
[21] Zeph. 1:12, cited 6 times as a sermon text in the *Journal*.
[22] Acts 3:26, cited 10 times as a sermon text in the *Journal*.
[23] I Peter 4:17-18; cited 18 times as a sermon text in the *Journal*.
[24] September 26, 1779; JLFA, I, 314.

acceptation, that Christ Jesus came into the world to save sinners; of whom I am chief." Asbury liked to take this text for his Christmas sermon, but it was also a favorite text otherwise.[25] Or he could base a call to new life upon:

If ye then, being evil, know how to give good gifts unto your children: how much more shall your heavenly Father give the Holy Spirit to them that ask him? [26]

For the Son of man is come to seek and to save that which was lost.[27]

Come unto me, all ye that labour and are heavy laden, and I will give you rest. Take my yoke upon you, and learn of me; for I am meek and lowly in heart; and ye shall find rest unto your souls. For my yoke is easy, and my burden is light.[28]

We then, as workers together with him, beseech you also that ye receive not the grace of God in vain. (For he saith, I have heard thee in a time accepted, and in the day of salvation have I succoured thee: behold, now is the accepted time; behold, now is the day of salvation.) [29]

Those who had found their glorious liberty he could urge along the way of holiness. Asbury had early concluded that there was little good in lamenting backsliding but much good in pressing to perfection. "Felt much power while preaching on perfect love. The more I speak on this subject, the more my soul is filled and drawn out in love. This doctrine has a great tendency to prevent people from settling on their lees." [30] II Peter 3:14 was a text Asbury outlined early in America.

I set out for Bohemia Manor; and though my body was much fatigued with my ride, and my head ached violently, yet in the

[25] I Tim. 1:15, cited 7 times as a sermon text in the *Journal*.
[26] Luke 11:13, cited 10 times as a sermon text in the *Journal*.
[27] Luke 19:10, cited 16 times as a sermon text in the *Journal*.
[28] Matt. 11:28-30, cited 14 times as a sermon text in the *Journal*.
[29] II Cor. 6:1-2, cited 24 times as a sermon text in the *Journal*.
[30] January 10, 1773; JLFA, I, 66.

evening I enforced these words: "Be diligent that ye may be found
of him in peace, without spot, and blameless;" and endeavoured to
show them, that in justification we have peace, in sanctification we
are without spot, and in perfect love we are blameless; and then
proceeded to show them wherein we must be diligent.[31]

He used II Peter, especially chapter 3, many times. As he grew
older he vowed to make every sermon a sermon on sanctification.
And he probably did it no matter what the text.

While Asbury's sermons were not strictly biblical in terms of
respect for the integrity of texts, they were biblical in the sense
that Asbury himself was saturated with Bible reading and study.
He was so steeped in the Bible and in Wesley's commentary on
the Bible that his exposition of the topics in his plan for salvation
had a very biblical cast. Illustrations were biblical; supporting
texts leapt to mind. He knew the Scriptures in such breadth that
there was always variety in his treatment of the standard topics
of his theology. He knew the whole of the Scriptures so well that
his adventures into allegory and prophecy did not unbalance him.

Some of his illustrations did not come from the Bible. These
were often selected current events given a homiletic overtone.
When he heard that scores of people in Philadelphia were dying of
"camp fever" every day, he said it seemed as if the Lord intended
to bring men to their proper reflections and duties by sword,
pestilence, and famine. If men would live rightly with God and
neighbor they could enjoy God's blessing rather than his curse.[32]
A certain Mr. R. of Asbury's acquaintance was a rich man who
became ill but got converted in time. The message was plain: All
living men had better listen and do likewise.[33] On the other hand,
a certain young man turned his back on the gospel and then suddenly died. This too was the judicial hand of God and a warning.[34]
Storms with thunder and lightning often brought vividly to Asbury the awful majesty of God and the hopelessness of the wicked.

[31] December 21, 1772; JLFA, I, 59.
[32] February 4, 1777; JLFA, I, 230.
[33] March 11, 1777; JLFA, I, 232.
[34] April 7, 1775; JLFA, I, 153.

"This day the thunder and lightning struck four people dead on the spot. Awful scene! And will man still venture to be careless and wicked? I made some improvement on the subject in the evening." [35]

When the Americans rose up in arms because some British marines came ashore to raid a print shop, Asbury observed:

> But if it is thought expedient to watch and fight in defence of our bodies and property, how much more expedient is it to watch and fight against sin and Satan, in defence of our souls, which are in danger of eternal damnation! [36]

He played on this theme all through the war. When the citizens turned out in fear for a fire alarm at 2:00 A.M., Asbury said, "What a resemblance of the general judgment! But, if the cry of fire alarms us, how much more shall we be alarmed by the archangel's trumpet!" [37] In some of these illustrations he sounds like an ancient prophet echoing the ancient wisdom of making every crisis a call to repentance. In some others he seems to repeat miracle tales of the credulous, especially those tales in which God vindicates the Methodists. [38]

Evidently Asbury was not the most popular of Methodist preachers, and he did not count himself a skilled preacher. He almost always recorded his impression of the response to his preaching. About half the time he counted the response tame indeed; it was a "dry" or "dull" or "heavy" time. For the better responses he spoke of a "stirring" or "shaking" or "moving" or "melting." Only rarely did he record any outbreak of "holy noise" under his preaching. On first impression the people would rather hear William McKendree or the popular Negro preacher, "Black Harry." Once when he was sick Asbury asked Jesse Lee to preach first and he exhorted briefly following. The people thought that Lee was the bishop; they said the bishop was fine but they did not

[35] July 28, 1774; JLFA, I, 125; cf. pp. 162, 163, 247.
[36] October 3, 1775; JLFA, I, 164.
[37] September 29, 1774; JLFA, I, 133.
[38] E.g., November 4, 1779; JLFA, I, 320.

like what the old man said who spoke afterward.[39] Asbury himself commented that the zealous conversation and prayers of layman Henry Gough moved and melted the hearts of the people more than his own preaching.[40]

Something like that is the testimony of his contemporaries. Marsden says, "His talents as a preacher were respectable." [41] Ezekiel Cooper defended Asbury against a charge of ambition by saying that if Asbury were ambitious he would not choose traveling companions who could preach better than he could. The fact that he did so is assumed.[42] Bangs summarizes:

> His talents as a preacher must be estimated in connection with those other duties which devolved upon him as the superintendent of the Church. It is said by those who had the privilege of hearing him in the vigor of manhood, before time and care had wrinkled his forehead, that he was deep and systematical in his discourses, ably and "rightly dividing the word of truth," fluent and powerful in his delivery, as well as remarkably pointed in his appeals to the consciences of his hearers. His attitude in the pulpit was graceful, dignified, and solemn; his voice full and commanding; his enunciation clear and distinct; and sometimes a sudden burst of eloquence would break forth in a manner which spoke a soul full of God, and like a mountain torrent swept all before it.
>
> I remember an instance of this in the city of Baltimore in 1808, while he was preaching on a Sabbath morning in the Eutaw-street church, in the presence of many members of the General Conference, and among others, the Rev. Mr. Otterbein sat by his side in the pulpit. . . .
>
> But though Bishop Asbury was thus able and systematic in his preaching in the earlier days of his ministry, as other duties accumulated, the cares of the superintendency multiplied, and his travels necessarily enlarged, it seemed impossible for him to give that

[39] Jacob Gruber, quoted in Tipple, *Francis Asbury*, p. 304.
[40] July 26, 1774; JLFA, I, 194.
[41] Joshua Marsden, *Poems on Methodism Embracing the Conference, or Sketches of Wesleyan Methodism: and American Methodism, A Plea for Unity* (Philadelphia: Sorin and Ball, 1848), p. 106.
[42] Tipple, *Francis Asbury*, p. 236.

attention to reading and study which is essential for a full development and vigorous exercise of the mental powers. Hence in his latter
days his manner of preaching changed—he was often quite un-
methodical in his arrangement—sometimes abruptly jumping, if I
may so express it, from one subject to another, intermingling anecdotes of an instructive character, and suddenly breaking forth in
most tremendous rebukes of some prevalent vice, and concluding
with an admonition full of point and pathos.[43]

Yet with one voice those who knew him spoke of an almost mys-
terious effectiveness of the bishop. His voice was excellent for both
speaking and singing. He was "deep" and "solemn"; there must
have been an awful intensity about his presence. He communicated
his seriousness. He "dealt closely" with the people and they received this as his ministry. His prayers caught up the congregation; at a conference or an ordination or a celebration of the Lord's
Supper he evidenced a combination of dignity and feeling which
was deeply moving. Because of his burning concern for these particular persons and this particular occasion, the repetition of episcopal functions did not become perfunctory. So his traveling companion Henry Boehm never wearied of him:

> I have heard him over fifteen hundred times. . . . There was a rich
> variety in his sermons. No tedious sameness; no repeating old stale
> truths. . . . I have heard him preach fifty ordination sermons, and
> they were among the most impressive I have ever heard.[44]

Traveling companion Nicholas Snethen agreed:

> But though his pulpit exhibitions were the admiration and delight
> of those who heard him the most frequently; yet it must be ad-
> mitted, that he was not in general so edifying to strangers. This
> was owing, in part, to his laconic and sententious style, and the fre-
> quent concealment of his method; and in part, also, to his natural
> impatience of minuteness and detail, which was always heightened

[43] Nathan Bangs, *A History of the Methodist Episcopal Church* (New York: Mason
and Lane. 1838), II, 398-99.
[44] Boehm, *Reminiscences, Historical and Biographical, of Sixty-Four Years in the
Ministry,* ed. Joseph Wakeley (New York: Carlton and Porter, 1865), p. 440.

by the pressure of disease. He belonged to that class of preachers, who are said to wear well; who, the oftener they are heard, the better they are liked.[45]

Asbury was a judge of preaching. When he went to Anglican services he generally recorded his impressions.

Attending at church, as usual, I heard Dr. ——— blow away on, "This is the day that the Lord hath made." He makes a strange medley of his preaching; though he delivers many good things, yet, for want of some arrangement of his ideas, all appears to be incoherency and confusion.[46]

Dr. Inglis, at St. Paul's, was on his old tedious subject of the Lord's supper. He cannot be at any great loss in saying the same thing over and over again so frequently.[47]

Went to Nottoway church, where Mr. Jarratt gave an excellent sermon on, "A man shall be a hiding-place." He was rather shackled with his notes.[48]

Even when he heard a good sermon from these churchmen, he lamented that they often lost the good effect of it by failing to exhort the people afterward.

He also judged the preaching of his Methodist traveling preachers. After hearing the exhortation of Isaac Rollins, which he thought "coarse and loud enough," he gave Rollins some advice which "he seemed willing to take." [49] Of one preacher named Joseph Cromwell, who could neither read nor write well, he wrote, "He is the only man I have heard in America with whose speaking I am never tired; I always admire his unaffected simplicity." [50] He felt it his prerogative to examine any Methodist preacher and to school him as there was opportunity.

[45] "A Discourse on the Death of the Reverend Francis Asbury," in Harlan L. Feeman, *Francis Asbury's Silver Trumpet* (Nashville: Parthenon Press, 1950), p. 130.

[46] August 14, 1774; JLFA, I, 127-28.

[47] November 13, 1774; JLFA, I, 137.

[48] May 16, 1780; JLFA, I, 351.

[49] December 27, 1772; JLFA, I, 61.

[50] February 1, 1780; JLFA, I, 333.

I have thought that the good bishop was the best reader of the holy Bible I ever heard. . . . It appeared to me that he laid the accent on every word, and the emphasis on every sentence, just where the Holy Spirit intended they should be. I once saw him call up a class of the senior preachers in conference, like a class in school, and gave them a chapter to read in course. (One of them told me afterward that he would rather have been called on to preach before five thousand people.) He [Asbury] said it was a shame, if not a sin, for a minister to read the Scriptures in a kind of whisper, or dull, monotonous tone, either in families or congregation.[51]

His Notes to the *Discipline* are delightfully precise in advising preachers to convince sinners of their danger, to set forth the atoning blood, to keep engagements and that on time, to be deeply serious, to be cautious of allegorizing, to avoid awkward gestures, to beware of writing for the press on the advice of a few enthusiastic friends.[52]

But he was at his best when he judged his own preaching. Detachment was no normal characteristic of Asbury. He was always completely involved and serious, or anguishing to be so. However, in this homiletical self-criticism, there are a few fine unguarded moments of candor and even of humor. Generally his characterizations of his preaching on almost any page of the *Journal* are brief; he "had liberty" or he "preached with power" or he "was shut up." But sometimes there is more.

I came to Richard Walters's—sixteen miles. Spoke on Coloss. i, 26-28. Had light, and spoke long.[53]

I preached at Edward White's on Luke iii, 6-9, with great liberty; not in much order, but useful to the people.[54]

Losing some of my ideas in preaching, I was ashamed of myself, and pained to see the people waiting to hear what the blunderer had to

[51] James Quinn, in *Christian Advocate and Journal*, June 23, 1841.
[52] *Discipline*, 1798, pp. 85-89.
[53] September 20, 1780; JLFA, I, 379.
[54] January 1, 1780; JLFA, I, 329.

say. May these things humble me, and show me where my great strength lieth! [55]

Preached twice—speaker and hearers too dull. Alas! [56]

Found Henry Fry preaching to about eighty people. I spoke after him on Luke xiii, 23-25: was fervent; but the people thought I must speak like thunder to be a great preacher. I shall not throw myself into an unnatural heat or overstrained exertions.[57]

I attempted to preach at Newton. I raged and threatened the people, and was afraid it was spleen.[58]

Bore a feeble testimony for nearly an hour.[59]

I attempted to preach at Bath, on "the lame and the blind:" the discourse was very *lame;* and it may be, I left my hearers as I found them—*blind.*[60]

I had very little life in preaching to a few dead souls.[61]

I spoke long and freely on the parable of the sower to four hundred people; but it appears as if sinners were Gospel-proof.[62]

Now that my mind is in a great measure lightened of its load of thought and labor for the conferences, I feel uncommon light and energy in preaching: I am not prolix; neither am I tame; I am rapid, and nothing freezes from my lips.[63]

He knew the limitations of preaching, his own as well as that of others. Unless it was followed by close application and supported by organization of the common life, it offered little hope. But a man could do no less than to preach, and to preach his best.

[55] September 18, 1774; JLFA, I, 131.
[56] June 28, 1784; JLFA, I, 461.
[57] October 13, 1780; JLFA, I, 383.
[58] June 20, 1784; JLFA, I, 460.
[59] June 1, 1794; JLFA, II, 16.
[60] August 17, 1788; JLFA, I, 578.
[61] December 23, 1787; JLFA, I, 556.
[62] October 22, 1780; JLFA, I, 384.
[63] July 5, 1807; JLFA, II, 545.

8

SUPERINTENDENT

When Francis Asbury came traveling and preaching, he knew what he wanted to find. In every place where there was a population he wanted to find a congregation of working Methodists. The nucleus of the congregation should be the class, the body of confessing Christians and committed Methodists at that place who were pressing on in pursuit of perfection. Some large places might have two or more classes; some might experiment with a smaller and more intense unit called a band. But one local class was what Asbury commonly knew on his rounds.

Every class had a class leader, one of the best men available from their own number. He might be a man of considerable preaching experience, or he might be a layman who had never spoken a word in public meeting outside this one fellowship. He was a man of real significance in the Methodist system—in effect, the local pastor, though he received no pay. He was responsible for the scheduling and conduct of the services held each week. Although he presided, it was generally expected that many members would assist in the preaching, exhorting, singing, and prayer.

But the class leader was the one who was to know every member of his class and exactly where that member was in his personal religious pilgrimage. He was to lead each member to examine himself and to measure his conduct by the Methodist General Rules. He was to labor at proper training for Methodist children. He was to rally his class for ministry to any member in sickness or crisis. He and his class were to attract and serve a constituency from which could come new professions of faith in Jesus Christ. They were the local representatives of Methodism.

The circuit rider was a full-time itinerant preacher, practically a professional revivalist. His territory was broad. Even when a mature circuit rider had a young assistant working with him, the local class might not receive a visit oftener than once a month. The circuit rider did not stay very long; he might have twenty to forty classes on his round. He appointed new class leaders, when that was needed, and laid out their duties for them. The people expected forceful preaching from the circuit rider, better than they produced among themselves. They hoped for revival and conversions every time he came. The watch night or the love feast or the sacramental service or the revival meeting would be timed to coincide with his arrival. After the preaching service the circuit rider would meet the class; he would take the roll from the class leader and call the names one by one, inquiring about the spiritual state of each. This was the place to face and resolve differences in family, neighborhood, or class. If the unity was close and warm, one or two might express the hope that they had received the blessing of entire holiness or perfect love.

So the circuit rider was always just departed or soon expected; his effect was both lingering and anticipated. No one preacher stayed on the circuit longer than two years, but another rider always followed on the appointed schedule. He preached, he exhorted, he disciplined, he carried books, he brought news. There was a wonderful dependability about the system. If a circuit rider was scheduled, one usually appeared. Not many things worked so well in the new land.

> Every thing is kept moving as far as possible; and we will be bold
> to say, that, next to the grace of God, there is nothing *like this* for
> keeping the whole body alive from the centre to the circumference,
> and for the continual extension of that circumference on every
> hand.[1]

If the circuit riders were effective and dependable, one big
reason was the presiding elder. Not all the preachers had been ordained as elders when the church was formed in 1784. Those who
were ordained elders were empowered to administer the sacraments.
As they visited their brethren for this purpose they exercised some
supervision as well. Even among the elders certain men were out-
standing and were considered responsible in a way for overseeing
their "district," though the area was poorly defined. Asbury took
this loose hierarchy and made it his finest tool as bishop. When he
was through shaping the presiding eldership, the whole of the
Methodist Episcopal Church was divided into districts. Within
each district a presiding elder was responsible for the operation of
his circuits, perhaps a dozen of them. It was his precise duty to
see that every circuit was manned and every appointed preaching
time kept. He supervised the traveling preachers in the same way
that a traveling preacher supervised the class leaders. So he rode
the circuits with his men periodically to teach them how to do
their work. When the presiding elder came with the circuit rider
to a local congregation, that was a big event indeed; the whole
church life quickened and more special services were scheduled to
coincide. Once every quarter all the district's traveling preachers,
local preachers, exhorters, and class leaders would meet with the
presiding elder as a group. Part of their work was reporting the
statistics of money and membership. Even more important was the
personal work done in talking out and resolving the tensions and
complaints of the workers. The presiding elder was the bishop's
man in his district. He applied the policy of the bishop and the
church, but he also served as a symbol of episcopacy to the people
and as a pastor to the preachers. Many Methodists might live and

[1] *Discipline*, 1798, p. 42; cf. pp. 72-83.

die without ever seeing the bishop. But they could see the bishop's man among them. Especially at the quarterly meetings in the summer there would be mass meetings of Methodists to hear all the district preachers at a big revival, to celebrate the love feast and sacraments, and to attend to the business of the church.[2]

Wherever Asbury went, he was chief shepherd of all this— taking the temperature of the organization at every level, examining the classes, keeping notes on the preachers in service, and keeping his eyes open wide to find more preachers to appoint. He was seeing to it that the presiding elders were "the guards of the body, the eyes of the bishop." He was spying out population movements and mapping new circuits in his mind. The thing he felt he had to do every year was to preside over the annual conference sessions where all the traveling preachers and presiding elders met. At these conferences only the full-time circuit riders were allowed; there were no class members or class leaders or local exhorters or local preachers. The traveling preachers had absolute control of the church in Asbury's time. If there was a quadrennial General Conference Asbury must attend that too. But during the time between conferences, and on the road from one conference to another, he dipped into Methodist life at every level as much as his energy allowed it.

Usually he traveled with an elder as a companion, an able preacher, perhaps conversant in German so he could preach in German pietist communities along the way. The presiding elder of the district he was visiting would often accompany. Within a circuit, the local circuit rider would bend his schedule to travel with the bishop. So Asbury commonly had quite an entourage in his later years. Large crowds would gather to hear so many giants of Methodism if the appointments were properly announced before. And whenever Asbury could time his visit to coincide with one of those quarterly meeting–revival–sacramental occasions of a

[2] William Warren Sweet, *The Rise of Methodism in the West: Being the Journal of the Western Conference, 1800-1811* (New York: Methodist Book Concern, 1920), pp. 42-43.

presiding elder, there was a religious festival indeed. Houses were not large enough to hold the crowds, and such events were often made into camp meetings.

I found the Lord was working among the people at Young's, in Mecklenburg, and felt myself to be in a warmer clime. We had a gracious time at quarterly meeting, especially at the sacrament: the words of our excellent sister Jones, both in speaking and in prayer, were sweetly and powerfully felt. The second day was great, both in preaching and love feast: my soul was melted; I have not witnessed such a meeting in the South.[3]

Saturday, 29. Our quarterly meeting began in the woods near Shepherdstown: we had about seven hundred people: I felt energy and life in preaching, and power attended the word. Brother Willis spoke, and the Lord wrought powerfully.

Sunday, 30. Was a high day—one thousand or fifteen hundred people attended; sinners began to mock, and many cried aloud; and so it went. I was wonderfully led out on Psalm cxlv, 8-12; and spoke, first and last, nearly three hours. O, how the wicked contradicted and opposed![4]

Asbury was inclined to think of his own word as final in the normal operation of Methodist affairs. There was a sort of an appeal possible, since the traveling preachers could bring any matter to the floor of annual conference or General Conference. Asbury was in theory amenable to the latter. But, in fact, the power and prestige of his person at these conferences was too much for a preacher to hope to overcome. Some opponents kept sniping away. They wanted to limit the authority of the bishop, elect the presiding elders, and allow preachers to locate with only three or four places to serve. These propositions coalesced in the mind of Asbury into one demonic Presbyterian heresy of operation and government. He would have none of it in his lifetime, and he died fighting it.

[3] March 28, 1786; JLFA, I, 510-11.
[4] August, 1789; JLFA, I, 607.

What bodies of Presbyterians there are in this country, all except Episcopalians, and these only in name, *local, local, local,* bishops and all. We might number, taking Baptists and Independents, 10 or 12 orders of them. And it is surprising that men amongst us, born Presbyterians, and fit to turn Arians, Socinians, or Pelagians to escape the principles of Presbyterianism, of Calvinism, should want more of their government amongst us than we have [illegible]. If we should let the elders choose the presiding elders, it will come to this: curtail a district into an old circuit, and a circuit (hardly work enough for 2 preachers) into 3 little parishes; cast off some places, keep four or five, attend these chiefly on Sabbath days, and be absent from your work at conferences three months. Beside, the good man must stay at home, day after day, like other lazy priests; yet the people must build not one, but 3 houses, and support 3 families. A presiding elder comes along and says, "Brethren, you neglect your work." They say, "Hush! we have families." [5]

So he ruled the conferences with an iron hand. He loved the church and the men; everybody knew that. He was praying for his preachers and raising money for them and sharing their lot without privilege. But when the decisions were made about what was best for the church and the men, he intended to make them. Nobody knew as much as he knew about all the churches and all the men, so he did all the stationing of preachers. If he asked information or opinion, he did not intend to be bound by it.

Mr. [James B.] Finley wrote in an after time some very interesting reminiscences of these times, and gives an incident of this Conference which was characteristic. "Bishop Asbury said to the preachers: 'Brethren, if any of you shall have anything peculiar in your circumstances that should be known to the superintendent in making your appointment, if you will drop me a note, I will, as far as will be compatible with the great interests of the Church, endeavor to accommodate you.' I had a great desire to go west, because I had relatives, which called me in that direction, and it would be more pleasant to be with them; so I sat down and ad-

[5] To Jacob Young, August 2, 1815; *Methodist History,* October, 1962, pp. 60-61.

dressed a polite note to the bishop, requesting him to send me west. My request was not granted. I was sent a hundred miles east. I said to him: 'If that's the way you answer prayers, you will get no more prayers from me.' 'Well, he said, be a good son, James, and all things will work together for good.' " [6]

Peter Cartwright had the same success.

When our appointments were read out, I was sent to Marietta Circuit. . . . This circuit extended along the north bank of the Ohio, one hundred and fifty miles, crossed over the Ohio River at the mouth of the Little Kanawha, and up that stream to Hughes River, then east to Middle Island. I suppose it was three hundred miles round. I had to cross the Ohio River four times every round.

It was a poor and hard circuit at that time. Marietta and the country round were settled at an early day by a colony of Yankees. At the time of my appointment I had never seen a Yankee, and I had heard dismal stories about them. It was said they lived almost entirely on pumpkins, molasses, fat meat, and bohea tea; moreover, that they could not bear loud and zealous sermons, and they had brought on their learned preachers with them, and they read their sermons, and were always criticizing us poor backwoods preachers. When my appointment was read out, it distressed me greatly. I went to Bishop Asbury and begged him to supply my place, and let me go home. The old father took me in his arms, and said, "O no, my son; go in the name of the Lord. It will make a man of you."

Ah, thought I, if this is the way to make men, I do not want to be a man. I cried over it bitterly, and prayed too. But on I started, cheered by my presiding elder, Brother J. Sale. [7]

It was his custom to announce the appointments to circuits and stations as the last item of conference business. As soon as the list was read he would mount his horse and ride away. The amazing thing was that he could make so many appointments so wisely and well. Henry Boehm observed him working at scores of conferences:

[6] George G. Smith, *Life and Labors of Francis Asbury* (Nashville: Publishing House of the M. E. Church, South, 1898), pp. 275-76.

[7] *The Autobiography of Peter Cartwright* (Centennial ed.; Nashville: Abingdon Press, 1956), p. 75.

He was wise and far-seeing, and kept his work planned and mapped out beforehand. The mass of the appointments were arranged before conference, so that but few changes needed to be made. . . . He had an almost intuitive knowledge of men. He would sit in conference and look from under his dark and heavy eyebrows, reading the countenances and studying the character and constitution of the preachers. He also kept a record of his observations upon men for his own private use. . . . He would say to me, "Henry, Brother A or B has been too long in the rice plantations, or on the Peninsula; he looks pale, health begins to decline; he must go up to the high lands." The preacher would be removed and know not the cause, and the next year come to conference with health improved and constitution invigorated. . . . The bishop assigned few reasons, and made but few explanations for his conduct.[8]

However, this kind of assignment by inspired executive hunch also caused much unrest.

Peopling the Methodist organization was Francis Asbury's constant work. He and his presiding elders were always enlisting and training preachers. He wooed the most promising. Peter Cartwright said that when he moved to Lewiston County, Kentucky, he asked his presiding elder for a letter of transfer as a Methodist member. What he received instead was a preacher's license and a commission to organize a new circuit. Asbury saw the possibilities of the brash young Cartwright, making him a traveling preacher at age nineteen and a presiding elder at age twenty-seven. Cartwright said he got his training to preach by riding the toughest frontier circuits and preaching. Out of the thousands of Methodist traveling and local preachers who were his contemporaries, he reported, "There were not fifty men that had anything more than a common English education, and scores of them not that; and not one of them was ever trained in a theological school or Biblical institute." [9] William McKendree also received Asbury's personal attention. McKendree had been in O'Kelly's district and had heard so much evil of Asbury and of episcopacy that he dropped out of

[8] Boehm, *Reminiscences,* pp. 439-40.
[9] *Autobiography,* p. 267.

the ministry when the O'Kelly schism occurred. Asbury gently persuaded McKendree to travel with him for a while without demanding recantation and without deciding the question of his future. McKendree was reclaimed for Methodism and actually succeeded Asbury as bishop.

Asbury also anguished over the failures among his ministers. His percentage of failure with preachers chosen for charismatic gifts seems to have been about the same as the percentage of failure in denominations with stricter educational requirements. Of the first four American preachers admitted by the Methodists, three ended wretchedly. Isaac Rollins, whom Asbury had counseled about his preaching, gave up Methodism and good character in favor of independency and whiskey. "Fallen, deceitful, self-deceiving man, I leave thee to God and thy own conscience," commented Asbury.[10] Joseph Cromwell, of whose plain preaching Asbury said he never tired, also tragically turned to drink.[11] Abraham Whitworth was expelled for intemperance: "A letter from Mr. Thomas Rankin brought melancholy tidings of Abraham Whitworth. Alas for that man! He has been useful, but was puffed up, and so fell into the snare of the devil. My heart pitied him: but I fear he died a backslider." [12]

Mostly he maintained the ranks of Methodist preachers by seeking the most promising from the host of young exhorters trained up in the classes with the manifest approval of their peers. The appeal of his organization certainly was not based on money. In the south and west there was an aversion to "paid" or "hireling" preachers. Part of this aversion was based in Wesleyan sectarian feeling against the Anglican clergy; part of it was based in the resentment of the American backwoodsman against the paid missionary from outside. Baptist farmer preachers preached without pay and made a virtue of it. The salaried Presbyterian and Congregational clergy generally counted themselves better than the unlettered frontiersmen and their homegrown preachers; these

[10] October 9, 1781; JLFA, I, 412; cf. p. 444 for a full account of Rollins' behavior.
[11] JLFA, I, 91 n.
[12] July 21, 1774; JLFA, I, 123.

eastern "sheepskin" men were always plotting to improve or reform the folk culture with schools and societies. This was very
hard for the frontier hyperdemocrats to take. So they did not pay
their preachers as a matter of principle. They gave a yearly "allowance"—if the money was at hand to pay it.

At first the allowance for a Methodist preacher was sixty-four
dollars per year, and he was expected to count any gifts or marriage fees from individuals against this amount. In 1800 the
amount was raised to eighty dollars per year and the requirement
of accounting for gifts was removed. All this was contingent on
there being money available at the conference to pay the allowance.
In 1802 only the Baltimore Conference was solvent; in the others
Asbury and his preachers got only their proportionate share of
whatever was there.[13] Cartwright said he received about forty
dollars in 1806 but that many of his colleagues did not receive
half that amount. [14]

Asbury grumbled some. "Our poor preachers keep Lent a great
part of the year here. Our towns and cities, at least our conferences,
ought not to let them starve for clothing." [15] Actually he did little
about it. Financial stewardship for the support of a ministry was
not a popular theme with the people, nor was it a compatible
theme for him. He started a personal "mite fund" to which Methodists who were willing could contribute for relief of poor preachers. He passed the hat among the poor preachers in behalf of other
preachers who were even poorer. He approved the use of profits
from the Methodist Book Concern to support poor preachers and
he willed his personal estate to this cause. He gave or loaned his
own money, when he had any, to destitute circuit riders. He helped
establish the "chartered fund" in 1796 for the relief of "distressed
travelling preachers, for the families of travelling preachers, and
for superannuated and worn out preachers, and the widows and

[13] Sweet, *Rise of Methodism*, pp. 46-48, 104, 144; Letter of John Dickins to Asbury
in William P. Strickland, *The Pioneer Bishop, or the Life and Times of Francis Asbury*
(New York: Carlton and Porter, 1858), p. 197.

[14] *Autobiography*, p. 74.

[15] To Thomas Morrell, July 3, 1793; JLFA, III, 120.

orphans of preachers." [16] But he seemed to think it unworthy to press the constituency for any real support for the preachers. He was himself a frequent complainer against the settled and salaried men.

Lord, have mercy upon the Reformed Churches! O ye dry bones, hear the word of the Lord! I was much obliged to my friend for renewing my clothing and giving me a little pocket money; this is better than £500 per annum. I told some of our preachers, who were very poor, how happy they were; and that probably, had they more, their wants would proportionately increase.[17]

As to the Presbyterian ministers, and all ministers of the Gospel, I will treat them with great respect, but I shall ask no favours of them: to humble ourselves before those who think themselves so much above the Methodist preachers by worldly honours, by learning, and especially by salary, will do them no good.[18]

And he wanted his church in no way beholden to rich Methodists.

Let all our Chapels be built plain and decent; but not more expensively than is absolutely unavoidable: Otherwise the Necessity of raising Money will make Rich Men necessary to us. But if so, we must be dependent upon them, yea, and governed by them. And then farewell to the Methodist-Discipline, if not Doctrine too.[19]

The support of our preachers, who have families, absorbs our collections, so that neither do our elders nor the charity school get much. We have the poor, but they have no money; and the worldly, wicked rich we do not choose to ask.[20]

His ideal was an army of preachers like himself—poor, unworldly, and celibate.

[16] Lee, *Short History*, p. 234.
[17] August 31, 1792; JLFA, I, 728.
[18] December 7, 1806; JLFA, II, 523.
[19] *Discipline*, 1785, p. 28.
[20] November 3, 1789; JLFA, I, 612.

Marriage was precisely the rock on which the system foundered. Asbury's preachers, being outgoing men and normally red-blooded creatures, fell in love and wished to marry. This required money. Further, husbands wanted to be home with their families more often than by a once-a-month appointment as they came round the circuit. Asbury solved the problem for himself. He would not marry.

If I should die in celibacy, which I think quite probable, I give the following reasons for what can scarcely be called my choice. I was called in my fourteenth year; I began my public exercises between sixteen and seventeen; at twenty-one I travelled; at twenty-six I came to America: thus far I had reasons enough for a single life. It had been my intention of returning to Europe at thirty years of age; but the war continued, and it was ten years before we had a settled, lasting peace: this was no time to marry or be given in marriage. At thirty-nine I was ordained superintendent bishop in America. Amongst the duties imposed upon me by my office was that of travelling extensively, and I could hardly expect to find a woman with grace enough to enable her to live but one week out of the fifty-two with her husband; besides, what right has any man to take advantage of the affections of a woman, make her his wife, and by a voluntary absence subvert the whole order and economy of the marriage state, by separating those whom neither God, nature, nor the requirements of civil society permit long to be *put asunder?* it is neither just nor generous. I may add to this, that I had little money, and with this little administered to the necessities of a beloved mother until I was fifty-seven: if I have done wrong, I hope God and the sex will forgive me: it is my duty now to bestow the pittance I may have to spare upon the widows and fatherless girls, and poor married men.[21]

However, his preachers married at a great rate. Then they "located" by scores and hundreds.

Marriage is honorable in all—but to me it is a ceremony awful as death. Well may it be so, when I calculate we have lost the travelling

[21] January 27, 1804; JLFA, II, 423.

labours of two hundred of the best men in America, or the world, by marriage and consequent location.[22]

On a certain occasion, when he [Asbury] heard that one of his favorites in the "thundering legion," was a captive fast bound in love's golden fetters, he exclaimed: "I believe the devil and the women will get all my preachers." [23]

Asbury mellowed a little toward marriage. In 1800 the General Conference allowed eighty dollars per year for a traveling preacher's wife or widow besides sixteen dollars for each child under seven and twenty-four dollars for each child between the ages of seven and fourteen. This amount was to be paid only if need was demonstrated and only if the money was available to the conference; it was paid with the same poor frequency as other conference obligations were met. Asbury could joke about marriage in a bitter kind of way.

I find the care of a wife begins to humble my young friend, and makes him very teachable: I have thought he always carried great sail; but he will have ballast now.[24]

Jonathan Jackson is married: O thou pattern of celibacy, art thou caught! Who can resist? [25]

But he never really gave in. The thought of settled and married preachers was always a nasty shock.

How hardly shall preachers who are well provided for maintain the spirit of religion! But here are eight young men lately married: these will call for four hundred dollars per annum, additional— so we go.[26]

---

[22] July 9, 1805; JLFA, II, 474.
[23] William W. Bennett, *Memorials of Methodism in Virginia* (Richmond: Published by the Author, 1871), p. 184.
[24] December 28, 1779; JLFA, I, 325.
[25] September 2, 1805; JLFA, II, 479.
[26] March 17, 1811; JLFA, II, 666.

Alas! what miseries and distresses are here. How shall we meet the charge of seventy married out of ninety-five preachers—children—sick wives—and the claims of conference? We are deficient in dollars and discipline.[27]

Our preachers get wives and a home, and run to their *dears* almost every night: how can they, by personal observation, know the state of the families it is part of their duty to watch over for good? [28]

So far as he was concerned, the really normative and ideal Methodist preacher should be wedded only to his work. His rightful place was always on the road.

Asbury lubricated the whole machinery of Methodism with his letters. He wrote down his thoughts even for those near at hand. For example, when he found that he and his fellow bishop McKendree actually had little time for conversation, he wrote a letter of counsel to him. But he also sent letters all over the church. There were contracts and official documents to be written and signed by the bishop's hand. There were troubleshooting letters to points of friction. There were letters of instruction in reply to queries. There were newsletters based on the reports always coming in from all over the church; as the settlers looked to their circuit rider for news, so the preachers and presiding elders looked to Asbury.

I have eighteen letters to answer, and more are no doubt on their way.[29]

Yesterday and to-day I have written fifteen letters.[30]

I am crowded with letters—have much reading and writing, and the temporal concerns of the college, and the printing to attend to.[31]

I have written to several of my ancient friends in Philadelphia. I may say of letters, as it was said of silver in the days of Solomon,

[27] May 25, 1815; JLFA, II, 781.
[28] June 17, 1810; JLFA, II, 639.
[29] December 17, 1809; JLFA, II, 623.
[30] August 11, 1811; JLFA, II, 683.
[31] June 19, 1790; JLFA, I, 642-43.

"I make no account of that:" I suppose I must write nearly a thousand in a year.[32]

Methodism, as envisaged and built by Francis Asbury, was a mighty marvel. Every denominational polity had a plan for expansion to the frontiers and for covering the ground of the new nation. But the Methodist system not only covered the ground, it filled the territory with classes, circuit riders, and presiding elders all awaiting the bishop's call. Local preachers moving west often formed local classes before the first circuit rider ever appeared; when the circuit rider came, these classes joyfully linked into his schedule.

Perhaps the toughest frontier of all for Methodism was New England. There were hundreds of Congregational churches there, one in every community. A few Baptists and Anglicans and Quakers hardly made a mark on the Congregational unity. People and clergy thought the area was well churched. But Asbury did not see how any place with so many Calvinists, so many rich churches, so many married and salaried clergy, so little holy noise, and so little drive to get on to perfect holiness could be churched. The New Englanders did not even know what a class or a love feast was! So Freeborn Garrettson did some pioneer work, and then Jesse Lee was given New England for his district. Their preaching and singing were a curiosity at first but, especially at Lynn, Massachusetts, where many were disaffected from their Congregational minister, they gathered enough seekers and displaced Congregationalists to form classes. Asbury made his first visit in 1791. New England always depressed him. He liked the good roads and the good cooking—except that they charged him for it—and the law and order. As for religion, he did not see much life in it up there. And the Congregationalists kept cooling off his Methodists.

It was the west which belonged especially to the Methodists. The swarming of settlers to the west came largely from the back

[32] January 21, 1796; JLFA, II, 76.

country of Virginia and North Carolina, both centers of strength for Methodism and reservoirs of young preachers. No other denomination of the middle colonies or of New England prepared realistically for the vast migration of settlers to the west. The Methodist Episcopal Church had both the drive for church extension and the preachers to satisfy it. The Methodists, with their system of manning and multiplying circuits, saw the need for ministry in the west and literally filled in the land. Francis Asbury was in his glory supervising it all, but he died when the taking of the west was just well begun. Nevertheless, the pattern was set by him and the first great steps made.

When Asbury became bishop in 1784 there had been eighty-three traveling preachers and a membership of just short of fifteen thousand. In 1815, the year before he died, the traveling preachers numbered more than seven hundred and the local preachers more than two thousand. Asbury gloried in a membership of

two hundred and twelve thousand, with possibly not one, but three millions of souls congregated in the year. Formerly, our people covered only three or five hundred miles, now scattered one thousand or fifteen hundred in width, three thousand in length! [33]

One big reason for the growth was the Methodist system of polity under Asbury. The other reason was revival.

[33] To Thomas L. Douglass, September 29, 1815; *Methodist History*, October, 1962, p. 56.

9

REVIVALIST

Revival did not begin with Francis Asbury, nor did it depend upon him. Where serious people are moved to think about ultimate questions of discipleship and destiny, results may go beyond the ordinary. There may be uncommon physical actions; there may be radical reorientation of persons; there may be some stage or combination of these. The religious man affirms that God's action preceding and during and after such intensive and decisive times may make of them a revival. A wide variety of means have been used to confront man with his need, to excite him in his quest, and to move him to decision. Preaching and prayer and song are the means most treasured by evangelical Christians.

Asbury knew about revivals before his own time, from Pentecost to the Puritans. On the ship, just before he set foot on the shore of the New World, he had written: "In America there has been a work of God: some moving first amongst the Friends, but in time it declined; likewise by the Presbyterians, but amongst them also it declined." [1] This was his recognition of the Great Awakening.

[1] September 12, 1771; JLFA, I, 4.

Jonathan Edwards had preached at Northampton until such a revival moved the town in 1734 that Edwards wrote his *Faithful Narrative of the Surprising Work of God, in the Conversion of Many Hundred Souls in Northampton, and the Neighbouring Towns and Villages*. The *Narrative* went through three editions and twenty printings by 1739; all New England was stirred. William Tennent, Sr., moved to a backwoods place called Neshaminy in Pennsylvania in 1727. There he drew on his own scholarship to train his boys and some sons of his neighbors for the ministry. Wherever the graduates of his "log college" ministered, revival seemed to stir. George Whitefield, a fiery composite of Anglicanism, Calvinism, and Methodism, crossed to America seven times and preached his way through the colonies stoking the fires of revival. He could be heard for a mile; he could touch the heart and the purse of Benjamin Franklin.

As Asbury saw it, this work of God in America, this "Great Awakening," had declined. John Wesley was the new prophet.

> The people God owns in England, are the Methodists. The doctrines they preach, and the discipline they enforce, are, I believe, the purest of any people now in the world. The Lord has greatly blessed these doctrines and this discipline in the three kingdoms: they must therefore be pleasing to him.[2]

But the doctrine and discipline of Methodism looked to revival too. Jonathan Edwards' *Narrative* had struck young John Wesley with terrific force.[3] Wesley wanted to hold fast to the Church of England, but he wanted the doctrine of the Church of England to be felt. Heart religion was the very stuff of Methodism; transformation was expected. Wesley said:

> I have seen (as far as a thing of this kind can be seen) very many persons changed in a moment from the spirit of fear, horror, despair, to the spirit of love, joy and peace, and from sinful desire till then

[2] *Ibid.*
[3] Albert Outler, ed., *John Wesley* (New York: Oxford University Press, 1964), p. 15.

reigning over them, to a pure desire of doing the will of God: him that was a drunkard and is now exemplarily sober: the whoremonger that was, who now abhors the very "garment spotted by the flesh." ... This is the fact; let any judge of it as they please.[4]

Wesley did not want noisy physical manifestations, but if there was noise it was only the devil resisting and so no grounds for letup.

Asbury's hope for a "work of God" in America was of one piece with the hope of the Great Awakening and the hope of Wesley and the hope of a host of evangelicals of the eighteenth century.[5] Personal renewal in revival was the mark of it. That was why he was so demanding in discipline on the congregations at Philadelphia and New York; nominal membership was not to be tolerated. That was why he kept probing and preaching and praying among the people outside the cities, recording the response of every gathering. That was why he loved the vigor of his work at Baltimore so well. That was why he found the work of Strawbridge exciting: "The Lord hath done great things for these people, notwithstanding the weakness of the instruments, and some little irregularities." He was always expectant for the "great work" and sniffing for the signs of it.

The greatest revival news which Asbury heard came from the parish of Devereux Jarratt. This man Jarratt was American born and a nominal member of the Church of England until he was converted under New Side Presbyterian preaching. He trained for the Presbyterian ministry but took ordination as an Anglican while in Engand in 1762. The next year he became Anglican rector in Dinwiddie County in Virginia. He was a thoroughgoing evangelical who livened the religious scene for fifty or sixty miles around—to the disgust of most of his Anglican cohorts. Just before the Revolution the Methodists reached Jarratt's area; Robert Williams, Joseph Pilmoor, and William Watters were the pioneers. The new Brunswick Circuit, as Williams formed it in 1774, reached

[4] Walter Russell Bowie, *Men of Fire* (New York: Harper & Row, 1961), p. 196.
[5] See A. Skevington Wood, *The Inextinguishable Blaze* (Grand Rapids: Eerdmans, 1960).

from Petersburg in Virginia to beyond the Roanoke in North Carolina.

Jarratt liked the Methodists from the start. They were kindred spirits. He encouraged his people to join Methodist societies, which he defended as part of his own Church of England. He preached for the Methodists and counseled them and administered the sacraments for them. The Methodists furnished the preachers and multiplied the meetings. Asbury entered fully into his ministry in the south in 1773. Jarratt reports, "In the counties of Sussex and Brunswick, the work, from the year 1773, was chiefly carried on by the labours of the people called Methodists." [6] So Asbury came south just as this work was warming. He had heard about the happy response to Methodist preaching in Virginia. He knew that the English missionary George Shadford had been sent there. Not until 1775 did he leave his own work in charge of local preachers and visit Brunswick Circuit himself. He smelled the smoke of revival as he approached: "God is at work in this part of the country; and my soul catches the holy fire already." [7] He correctly sensed the vitality; within two years of the founding of Brunswick Circuit nearly one third of the total Methodist membership of the colonies was in it.

Jarratt and Asbury become firm friends during this 1775 visit, though the friendship was to have hard days to endure. When the Methodists formed themselves into a church in 1784 Jarratt was given no advance warning. For years he had been defending and serving Methodists as nothing other than part of the Church of England. Now the Methodists had broken clear from the old church and had taken over for themselves the lively work they had furthered in his parish. Now they quit coming to visit him and stopped seeking his counsel. Now they condemned slavery, and Jarratt was a slaveholder. He penned some bitter feelings about Methodist conduct and about Asbury in the years immediately follow-

[6] Devereux Jarratt, "A Brief Narrative of the Revival of Religion in Virginia"; JLFA, I, 209.
[7] November 2, 1775; JLFA, I, 166.

ing 1784.[8] Yet he could not but love Methodist evangelicalism, and by 1791, especially after an apology and friendly visit from Coke in that year, happy relations were restored. It was Asbury who preached a funeral sermon. "He was the first who received our despised preachers—when strangers and unfriended, he took them to his house, and had societies formed in his parish." [9]

Asbury was even more closely drawn into friendship with Shadford. Here was a man who could take the incipient revival in Brunswick Circuit and develop it as a flaming tool of evangelism. Even a hostile writer seems to give him grudging praise:

> The revival reached its peak with the arrival of George Shadford, who apportioned the territory and sinners among himself and the local preachers and set to work with great energy. There was almost continuous preaching throughout the length and breadth of Brunswick circuit, and that part of Virginia became the scene of the most remarkable religious excitement the continent had seen since the labours of Jonathan Edwards in New England. The war was forgotten while vast multitudes attended the meetings in the chapels, in private homes, and in the fields, and by the end of the year 1800 new members had been added to the Methodist societies. All of the services were attended by miracles, and by the curious physical manifestations and emotional excesses so characteristic of methodistic religion.[10]

Shadford was evidently a superb preacher. Yet he took time enough to be a warm friend to Asbury, a man not easy to love.

It may be that Asbury's happiest hours were those he spent at revival labors in teamwork with Shadford. Certainly the religious vitality of Brunswick Circuit became a kind of norm. Methodism in America should be like that. Asbury was intoxicated by this full-bodied form of American revival; from now on he would

[8] Devereux Jarratt, *The Life of the Reverend Devereux Jarratt* (Baltimore: Warner and Hanna, 1806), pp. 114-24, 156-59, 180-81.

[9] April 19, 1801; JLFA, II, 291-92; cf. Sweet, *Virginia Methodism*, pp. 109-17.

[10] Herbert Asbury, *Methodist Saint*, pp. 96-97.

always want more noise than Wesley or Coke. When Jarratt's "Brief Narrative of the Revival of Religion in Virginia" came to him in 1776 he copied it verbatim into his Journal.[11] Later he copied Rankin's letter to Wesley about this same revival in Virginia, complete with its detailed record of the scores of hearers being struck down under conviction so that their groans and cries drowned out the preaching. Many who were struck down were soon to be lifted up with tears of joy and shouts of victory. All this was an inspiration for his own work in Delaware during his time of exile during the war; the result was 1,800 Methodists added to the societies in the area where he was able to work during those exile years.

During the whole of his service in America, Asbury served as a kind of information center for Methodism through his letters. The news he liked best to receive was news of revival. The news he trumpeted across the church was news of revival. The revival in Virginia did not end in 1775. It went on with substantial strength, coming to another great crescendo in 1785 and 1786. Again at the turn of the century the revival of religion was almost universal in America. On every round of the land as bishop, Asbury was refreshed by evangelical outbursts at many points. His aim was to spread the revival fervor so far as he could. Virginia was his standard rather than New England. Revival was necessary, right, and good.

So it is no wonder that Francis Asbury quickly noted the camp meeting, adopted it, promoted it, regularized it, and made it his own. He and the camp meeting were made for each other. Field preaching and outdoor meetings were common enough in Methodist history and in American experience. However, the camp meeting was something special, a creature of the American woods. For several reasons it had become a frontier custom to celebrate the Lord's Supper infrequently, even for faithful Christians as seldom as once or twice a year. These rare sacramental occasions were extended to be long and serious. They involved the services

[11] December 19, 1776; JLFA, I, 207-19.

of two or more ministers, much preaching, and intense preparation over a period of three or four days. Large crowds gathered. When the crowds exceeded the room under roof, temporary camping provisions were made for the overflow. People of several religious persuasions might attend; Presbyterian, Methodist, and Baptist combinations were most common.

The noisy and hearty frontier revival invaded these sacramental occasions. In Kentucky, Presbyterian revivalist James McGready planned a sacramental occasion at his church at Gasper River for July of 1800. He invited Methodist preachers John Page and John McGee. So many people came that the church and neighborhood could not feed or house them. Religious excitement ran high from the first night's meeting, and the aroused people did not wish to go home. This happened at other places too. Beginning in 1801 they came prepared to camp and to cook and to stay. The most notorious of the early camp meetings was held at Cane Ridge in Bourbon County, Kentucky. The camp eclipsed the church; the revival eclipsed the sacrament. Asbury soon had word of it.

> The work of God is running like fire in Kentucky. It is reported that near fifteen if not twenty thousand were present at one Sacramental occasion of the Presbyterians; and one thousand if not fifteen hundred fell and felt the power of grace.[12]

The Presbyterians had neither the manpower nor the stomach for the primitive camp meeting. They divided rather quickly into some who were for it and others who were against it. Though they discussed it considerably they were not in position to marshal or to man it. So they made limited use of the camp meeting so far as it fitted their parish or mission plan. Asbury commented:

> Report says there was a mighty falling among the Presbyterians, but it is reported they are without conviction or conversion, some at least. They say the elders go among them and hold the candles but they will not or cannot say anything to the distressed.

[12] To Mrs. John Dickins, September 12, 1801; JLFA, III, 226.

They want God to work alone. They want God to work without man or means except preaching and ordinance to see if his work is real. The people report they bark and snatch, and make strange noises. No wonder if they are left poor souls to themselves to contend with the devil and sin, and sinners. Mark, these are only reports. I think it is either judicially come upon these people or it is because they are come to the birth and there is not strength to bring forth for them and the people, that are stricken, educated in the doctrine that they can do nothing, they will not attempt to do anything.[13]

Baptists lacked the regional organization to plan camp strategy and they lacked the itinerant giants to man the preaching stands. Asbury and the Methodists were ready.

Asbury had the big vision. "God hath given us hundreds in 1800, why not thousands in 1801, yea, why not a million if we had faith. 'Lord increase our faith.'"[14] He and his preachers were not afraid of the noise and intensity of revival; it was their element. They had been exporting revival from Virginia and Maryland and Delaware all along, and now, by God's grace, new centers and new means were at hand. Asbury's preachers were close to the frontier folk, especially to the southern population stream now settling much of the west. They could communicate. The experience on the circuits had taught them how to move a crowd and had given them a repertory of revival sermons.

Added to this was the happy arrangement of combining camp meetings with regular conferences of Methodist ministers. If there were to be conferences, let the preachers hold the summer conference sessions at a camp. Thus all the preachers could preach, hear others preach, conduct love feasts, administer sacraments, stir up revival, and serve the religious interests of the large rural population around the campgrounds.

My [McKendree's] Spring visit ended at our old friend Philip Gatche's, Little Miami, on the third Sunday in June, which was the thirteenth Sabbath in continuity that I attended meetings from two

---

[13] To George Roberts, August 18, 1803; JLFA, III, 269.
[14] To Stith Mead, January 20, 1801; JLFA, III, 196.

to four days each. Our congregations were generally large, (in places where fifty formerly made a respectable congregation, a thousand is now a tolerable gathering) and blessed be God we were generally favoured with distinguishing marks of the divine presence. . . . People came from far to the Miami quarterly meeting. I heard of women that walked thirty miles to it.[15]

The year 1806 has produced great changes in the natural and political world—but in America it is in the spiritual world! Stith Mead, from the Richmond District, from March to August, 400 converted and a number sanctified. Shands built houses or huts for camp meetings, and lived nearly 100 days and nights in the woods till November. Brother Chandler, 150 days and nights in the woods, from May 3 to November, 1806. From May to August 29, converted 5368, sanctified, 2805, in the Delaware District. Somerset camp meeting, converted, 1165, sanctified, 606. Dover campmeeting, converted, 123; sanctified, 919.

Oh, my brother, when all our quarterly meetings become campmeetings, and 1000 souls should be converted, our American millennium will begin. And when the people in our towns and country assemble by thousands, and are converted by hundreds, night after night, what times! Lord, increase our faith. Nothing is too hard for him who made and redeemed a world.[16]

His implicit faith in the camp meeting made Asbury sure it should be used everywhere. It was not just for the woods. It was for Pittsburgh and Baltimore and Long Island and New England and Virginia. He made the camp meeting move from west to east against the population stream.[17] To the presiding elder of Pittsburgh District he wrote:

I wish you would also hold campmeetings; they have never been tried without success. To collect such a number of God's people to-

[15] Francis Asbury, *Extracts of Letters, Containing Some Account of the Work of God Since the Year 1800* (New York: Cooper and Wilson, 1805), pp. 40-41.

[16] To Thornton Fleming, November 7, 1806; JLFA, III, 356-57.

[17] See HAM, I, 517-19.

gether to pray, and the ministers to preach, and the longer they stay, generally, the better—this is field fighting, this is fishing with a large net.[18]

And to the minister of a large church in Baltimore;

I wish most sincerely that we could have a campmeeting at Duck Creek out in the plain south of the town, and let the people come with their tents, wagons, provisions and so on. Let them keep at it night and day, during the conference; that ought to sit in the meeting.[19]

From the beginning the camp meeting was subject to serious abuses. Its enemies could cite them; its friends equally deplored them. Social delinquents attended the meetings, often bent on mischief. The excitement and removal of restraint sometimes undid the more stable. Asbury, the champion of the camp meeting, was at the same time Asbury, the enemy of disorder. But where is the point at which disorder begins? There had to be room for liveliness; "for you know we American Methodists pray, and preach, and sing and shout aloud." [20] Asbury would have been sorely disappointed had there been no "holy noise." He wanted camp meetings to "shake the formality of religion out of the world," [21] but the conduct of the whole meeting must stay firmly in the hands of the preachers and officers. That was the test.

My continual cry to the Presiding Elders is, order, order, good order. All things must be arranged temporally and spiritually like a well disciplined army.[22]

I judge you will find it best to have two stands. If the work should break out at one, you can go to another. I wish you to be singularly careful of order: sixteen or twenty men as watchmen, to have their hours of watching. I would have them to bear long, white,

[18] To Thornton Fleming, December 2, 1802; JLFA, III, 251.
[19] To George Roberts, December, 1802; JLFA, III, 255.
[20] To Coke, May 2, 1809; JLFA, III, 407.
[21] To Stith Mead, July 15, 1805; JLFA, III, 322.
[22] To Thomas Sargent, December 28, 1805; JLFA, III, 333.

peeled rods, that they may be known by all the camp, and be honored. Let them be the most respectable elders among the laity.[23]

He heard echoes of his call for orderly procedures from the field.

> July 24, the day previous to the beginning of our campmeeting, I was with our brethren, on the camp-ground, making arrangements. . . . Thursday, July 25, at sun-rise, the trumpets gave the signal for morning prayer; after which the people began to assemble from different quarters. At eight o'clock, the trumpets sounded the signal for public preaching: when the rules of the meeting were read.
>
> Brother J. Lee took the stand, and preached from Isaiah xxxiii, 13. Brother J. Chalmers exhorted after him. The work broke out, and went on until the trumpets blew for preaching at three o'clock; but every thing was as orderly thro' the camp as in a Court of Justice.[24]

If the Enemy invaded the camp meetings, that called for resistance to the Enemy, not resistance to the preaching and the godly work. "All earth and hell is roused against field meetings, but we will endure fines, imprisonment, and death sooner than we will give them up." [25]

Asbury never saw them wane. Every year of his life there were more. In 1809 he said he hoped to see six hundred camp meetings the next year. "Campmeetings, campmeetings. Oh Glory, Glory!" [26] He suggested that some camping sites establish more permanent facilities with floors and roofs for major buildings. He saw the growth of explicit bodies of camp rules to be read at the first session of the meetings. He even heard some of his preachers complain about camping out through a whole conference and about feeling torn between their duty to conference and their duty to the altar of the penitents. But on the camps went, from strength to strength. And on Asbury went, from revival to revival, hearing reports of and glorying in those which he could not attend.

[23] To Daniel Hitt, August 22, 1804; JLFA, III, 300.
[24] From William P. Chandler, August 5, 1805; JLFA, III, 330.
[25] To Stith Mead, July 30, 1807; JLFA, III, 370.
[26] To Jacob Gruber, August 6, 1809; JLFA, III, 411.

10
EDUCATOR

Schooling was not Francis Asbury's strength. Nor does he seem to have been sensitive about his lack of formal education. There are few apologies. Especially when he was irritated with New England he could blast the claims of the educated.

Occasion was given to-day for expressions of wonder by a clerical character, that any one should be able to preach who had not acquired learning. What Jesuitical stupidity was here manifested! [1]

Never have I seen any people who would talk so long, so correctly, and so seriously about trifles. [2]

Here is college-craft, and priest-craft. [3]

Every candid inquirer after truth will acknowledge, upon reading Church history, that it was a great and serious evil introduced, when

[1] June 30, 1786; JLFA, I, 516.
[2] July 22, 1791; JLFA, I, 689.
[3] June 18, 1811; JLFA, II, 676.

philosophy and human learning were taught as a preparation for a Gospel ministry.[4]

It is said that there is a special call for learned men to the ministry; some may think so, but I presume a simple man can speak and write for simple, plain people, upon simple, plain truths.[5]

Such surges of resentment would only draw him closer to a substantial majority of his American constituents. They were largely untrained. In Asbury's day only the elite in the south went to school because the schools were private and they were scarce. Common men were likely to be suspicious of formal learning; they were without zeal or money to support it.

Nevertheless, Asbury was a son of Wesley. British Methodism had learned leaders. The Wesleys and Whitefield and Fletcher were university men. Wesley aimed for every Methodist to be a reader.

It cannot be that the people should grow in grace unless they give themselves to reading. A reading people will always be a knowing people. A people who talk much will know little. Press this upon them with all your might; and you will soon see the fruit of your labours.[6]

Methodist preachers, above all, should study. Wesley himself saw to it that there was plenty to read.

Theological essays, Wesley's own translations or versions of the Old and New Testaments (along with explanatory notes), sermons, and tracts were available everywhere and always in the Methodist societies. In addition there were diaries of interesting people, journals of Wesley and other leaders in the movement, volumes of poetry, hymns, biography, and history—always volumes of history.[7]

[4] December 14, 1805; JLFA, II, 488.

[5] William L. Duren, *Francis Asbury; Founder of American Methodism and Unofficial Minister of State* (New York: The Macmillan Company, 1928), p. 70.

[6] To George Holder, November 8, 1790; LJW, VIII, 247.

[7] HAM, I, 25.

There were fifty-six volumes in the *Christian Library* which he edited. Wesley not only got the material out, he got it read. He and his Anglican cohorts and his more mature preachers were always testing the lay preacher and pressing him on.

If Asbury was no Wesley, he had at least been on the receiving end of Wesley's educational thrust. He had to note the ignorance and wildness of many in the new land. He had to deplore the ignorance of his preachers, and even more their willingness to continue in the ministry without much improvement. But his standard was not the Oxford norm of Wesley. It was the norm of his own lay education obtained in the briefest of schooling and in Methodist service. If only one could teach the rudiments, provide the books, and inspire the discipline to study, it would be enough.

His concern for teaching the rudiments to the colonists appears early. Basic reading and writing will "give the key of knowledge in a general way." [8] Beyond that he was thinking about a Methodist school for boys, a good but modest secondary institution patterned after Wesley's Kingswood School in England. He discussed such a plan with Samuel Magaw in November of 1779 [9] and with John Dickins in June of 1780.[10] Asbury was especially concerned about the sons of Methodist preachers. If there must be married preachers, at least their boys should be spared the hazard of being educated in a home without the regular supervision of a father. Promising orphan boys were also to be prime candidates for the school. Asbury had an additional motivation; he dared to hope that a lot of fine Methodist preachers would emerge from such a school.

Asbury's school plan took an interesting direction when Thomas Coke arrived in 1784. Coke also wanted a school. However, the model in the mind of university man Coke was that of a degree-granting college to take its place with the elite of the academic world. The two men agreed on the location of the school, Abingdon in Maryland, some twenty-five miles outside Baltimore. They

[8] To the United Societies, September 16, 1791; JLFA, III, 102.
[9] JLFA, I, 324.
[10] JLFA, I, 358.

agreed with the conference on the name of the school, Cokesbury
College, thus embodying both their names. They received the approval of the Christmas Conference to proceed with the plan, it
being understood that the bishops would raise the needed money.
It is not clear whether they were ever of one mind about what
the school was to be. Perhaps in their enthusiasm they dared to
hope the rising institution would be so grand it would fulfill all
the hopes of both.

Asbury carried a heavy part of the burden of the institution
from the beginning. With Coke he circulated a subscription list
among the preachers and richer Methodists, raising the encouraging
sum of five thousand dollars. With this he and Coke bought building materials and six acres of land. When construction of the two-
story building began, he laid the cornerstone with a sermon on Ps.
78:4-8. When the school opened and was dedicated in 1787, he
preached three days in the chapel. In that year he and Coke produced a prospectus for the college to describe its work and to help
to raise funds.

> The Students will be instructed in English, Latin, Greek, Logic,
> Rhetoric, History, and as soon as the proper instruments or Appa-
> ratus can be procured, in Geography, natural Philosophy and Astron-
> omy. To these Languages and Sciences shall be added, when the
> Finances of our College will admit of it, the Hebrew, French,
> and German Languages.[11]

Orphans and sons of preachers were not to pay for board, clothes,
or instruction. For others, "the 10/. a Year for Tuition, we are
persuaded, cannot be lowered, if we give the Students that finished Education which we are determined they shall have." [12]

The primary business of the enterprise was religious formation
of the student; all the faculty, staff, and visitors were to work
toward this. Children were received as early as age seven because
"we wish to have the Opportunity of 'teaching their young ideas

---

[11] "An address to the Annual Subscribers for the Support of Cokesbury College";
JLFA, III, 55.
[12] *Ibid.*, p. 57.

how to shoot.' " [13] Even allowing for the influence of the rigidity of Kingswood School and of Asbury's own unhappy school days, he wrote a remarkable severity into the "Rules for the Economy of the College and Students."

1. The Students shall rise at five o'Clock in the Morning, Summer and Winter, at the ringing of the College-Bell.
2. All the Students, whether they lodge in or out of the College, shall assemble together in the College at six o'Clock, for public Prayer, except in Cases of Sickness; and on any Omission shall be responsible to the President.
3. From Morning-Prayer till Seven, they shall be allowed to recreate themselves as is hereafter directed.
4. At seven they shall Breakfast.
5. From Eight till Twelve, they are to be closely kept to their respective Studies.
6. From Twelve to Three, they are to employ themselves in Recreation and Dining:—Dinner to be ready at One o'Clock.
7. From Three till Six, they are again to be kept closely to their Studies.
8. At Six they shall Sup.
9. At Seven there shall be public Prayer.
10. From Evening-Prayer till Bed-time they shall be allowed Recreation.
11. They shall all be in Bed at Nine o'Clock, without fail.
12. Their Recreations shall be Gardening, Walking, Riding and Bathing, without Doors; and the Carpenter's, Joiner's, Cabinet-maker's or Turner's Business, within Doors. . . .
18. The Students shall be indulged with nothing which the World calls *Play*. Let this Rule be observed with the strictest Nicety; for those who play when they are young, will play when they are old.[14]

Asbury later realized this severity. *"That matter might have been managed better,"* he said. "We were to have the boys to become all angels!" [15]

[13] *Ibid.*, p. 55.
[14] *Ibid.*, pp. 58-59.
[15] November 1, 1804; JLFA, II, 445.

By the time the legislature of Maryland agreed to charter the school as a degree-granting college it was so near dead that there was ground for Asbury and Coke to wonder if it should be chartered at all. One thing was constant: the school was always deeply in debt. Asbury was always raising money for it in the conferences and among his friends and out of his own pocket. He was worried because the salaries of the school's employees were far in arrears and because some incendiaries had once tried to burn the building. He was at Charleston, South Carolina, when he got the news it was gone.

> We have now a second and confirmed account that Cokesbury college is consumed to ashes, a sacrifice of £10,000 in about ten years! The foundation was laid in 1785 and it was burnt December 7, 1795. Its enemies may rejoice, and its friends need not mourn. Would any man give me £10,000 per year to do and suffer again what I have done for that house, I would not do it. The Lord called not Mr. Whitefield nor the Methodists to build colleges. I wished only for schools—Doctor Coke wanted a college.[16]

Asbury looked on the end of the whole college experiment with weariness and relief. However, Dr. Coke stepped in to rally the forces to rebuild. With the help of a committee of Methodist men in Baltimore he raised four thousand dollars and promises of more if the school would be located there. They bought a huge dance hall next door to the Light Street Methodist Church and converted it into the new Cokesbury College with a much enlarged enrollment. One biographer says they must have forgotten to call off those Methodist imprecations long invoked against the place as a dance hall.[17] Just less than one year after the new college opened, both the college and the church were destroyed by fire! "It affected my mind," wrote Asbury, "but I concluded God loveth the people of Baltimore, and he will keep them poor, to

[16] January 5, 1796; JLFA, II, 75.
[17] Herbert Asbury, *Methodist Saint*, p. 172.

make them pure; and it will be for the humiliation of the society." [18]

That was the end of Asbury's vision of one school to serve and be supported by the whole church. From now on he returned to his policy of encouraging local Methodists to provide the rudiments of education in their own areas. Sometimes he advocated parochial schools for elementary education, as in 1791 when he encouraged "every large society, where the members are able and willing" to found a school for boys and a separate one for girls where the fundamentals of learning and religious life would be offered.[19] Sometimes he spoke of schools for a larger unit, such as "district schools" in 1793.[20] The fact seems to be that any proposal for a Methodist school, elementary or secondary, would merit his episcopal judgment and very likely his helping hand. So he shared in the establishment of Ebenezer Academy in Brunswick County, Virginia; Bethel Academy in Jessamine County, Kentucky; Bethel Academy in Newberry County, South Carolina; Cokesbury School in Davie County, North Carolina; Union Seminary at Uniontown, Pennsylvania; and others as well.[21]

Jesse Lee's comment about the district schools applied as well to the academies: "But most of them fell through in a few years; and at present they are hardly worth noticing in this history." [22] Every school which Asbury helped to found died in short order. Even his religious heavy-handedness can hardly bear all the blame for such a record. The history of each school is a sad story of nonsupport by the people. No Methodist schools were founded from 1793 until Asbury's death in 1816. The new shape of the future soon appeared in an action of the General Conference of 1820: "That it be, and is hereby recommended to all the annual conferences, to establish, as soon as practicable, literary institutions, under their own control, in such way and manner as they

---

[18] December 30, 1796; JLFA, II, 111.

[19] To the United Societies, September 16, 1791; JLFA, III, 102-3.

[20] Lee, Short History, p. 196.

[21] William Warren Sweet, Methodism in American History (Nashville: Abingdon Press, 1954), p. 211; HAM, I, 269-72; Herbert Asbury, Methodist Saint, p. 173.

[22] Short History, p. 196.

may think proper." [23] The location, foundation, and operation of schools was to be left to the conferences. This may have been the logical outcome of Asbury's experience, but he never came to enunciate any such policy of freedom from his own episcopal control. His belief was that Methodist schools were primarily places where young people were made intensely religious. He had his own convictions about the ways in which this must be done.

If he was not having his way in founding healthy weekday schools, how about a plan for teaching the rudiments of education in Sunday schools? Eighteenth-century Sunday schools were largely engaged in teaching reading, writing, and spelling. Compared to a school like Cokesbury College, they were distinctly more secular. The instruction was done on Sunday not because the undertaking was especially holy but because that was the only day the pupils had off from work. Still, the program looked like a natural for the interests of Methodism, and expressions of Asbury's desire for Sunday schools soon appeared.

What can be done for the instruction of poor children (whites and blacks) to read? Let us labour, as the heart and soul of one man, to establish Sunday schools in, or near the place of public worship. Let persons be appointed . . . to teach (gratis) all that will attend, and have a capacity to learn; from six o'clock in the morning till ten; and from two o'clock in the afternoon till six: where it does not interfere with public worship.[24]

But let us labour *among the poor* in this respect, as well as among the competent. O if our people in the cities, towns, and villages were but sufficiently sensible of the magnitude of this duty, and its acceptableness to God—if they would establish sabbath-schools, wherever practicable, for the benefit of the children *of the poor*, and sacrifice a few public ordinances every Lord's-day to this charitable and useful exercise, God would be to them instead of all the means they lose; yea, they would find, to their present comfort and the in-

[23] *Journals of the General Conference of the Methodist Episcopal Church, 1796-1836* (New York: Carlton and Phillips, 1855), p. 208.

[24] *Minutes . . . 1773-1794*, p. 147.

crease of their eternal glory, the truth and sweetness of those words, "Mercy is better than sacrifice." But there is so much of the cross in all this! O when shall we be the true followers of a crucified Saviour? [25]

He found himself facing four obstacles which kept the Methodist Sunday school from developing as a significant tool of education for the unlearned. First, there were not many illiterate or semiliterate Americans who were ready for such a regimen; on their day off they would rather fight or go hunting. Second, there were not many volunteer lay people who were willing to pour eight hours per week plus oceans of energy into a work with so little prestige. Third, some stout and noisy opponents of Sunday schools attacked them as desecrations of the Lord's day, as fomenters of social disorder offering education to poor whites and to Negroes, and as agents of Yankee imperialism who thought God's natural woodspeople needed improvement by learning. Fourth, Asbury and his preachers were so concerned for religious instruction that they kept moving in to take over the Sunday schools for this purpose rather than for teaching reading and writing. Asbury was among those pressing for more religious content; he urged John Dickins to prepare a *Short Scriptural Catechism* for use with the children to supplement available Wesleyan materials. Under these conditions the Sunday school sessions were to dwindle to a one-hour combination of pious exercise and religious instruction. Asbury appears as an interested but marginal figure in the early Sunday school movement. Jesse Lee's laconic comment on early Methodist Sunday schools for general education also tells the tale.

After this, Sunday schools were established in several places, and the teachers took nothing for their services. The greater part of the scholars were black children, whose parents were backward about sending them; and but few of them were regular in attending, and in a short time the masters were discouraged, and having no

[25] *Discipline,* 1798, p. 105.

pay, and but little prospect of doing good, they soon gave it up, and it has not been attended to for many years.[26]

Francis Asbury was not equipped to do the work of educational writing and publishing for American Methodists which his mentor Wesley had done for the English societies. Asbury could read better than he could write; his style had power but was always rough. So he was more a consumer and critic of literature than a large contributor to it. His episcopal duties and the limitations of the raw new land prevented scholarly labors. When there was any time to write, his letters and his *Journal* must always come first. In connection with his conference duties there was much writing for the Minutes and the *Discipline*. It is remarkable that he attended to all these so faithfully.

He did have some writing projects in mind. For example, he wrote poetry and once toyed with the idea of publishing a volume of it. Since German Reformed pastor Philip Otterbein was a close friend, Asbury tried the poems on him. Otterbein said, "Brother Asbury, I fear you was [sic] not born a poet." Asbury burned the manuscript and none of his verse remains. He began a *Short History of the Methodists* but did not complete it. He marked about three hundred pages of Baxter's *Reformed Pastor* for a reprint but was unable to see the project through.[27] He did complete and circulate a collection of sermons for the preachers.[28]

It was his opinion that the *Pocket Hymn-Book* was better suited to European Methodists than to Americans, so he compiled *A Selection of Hymns from Various Authors, Designed as a Supplement to the Methodist Pocket Hymn-Book*. Most of the hymns in Asbury's *Supplement* were from Charles Wesley and Isaac Watts; one notable addition was a new section of thirty-nine hymns on "Sanctification of Believers and Gospel Perfection," a completely new category. The book was issued in 1808. Asbury said in the preface:

[26] *Short History*, p. 161.

[27] Herbert Asbury, *Methodist Saint*, p. 283; Horace M. DuBose, *Francis Asbury; A Biographical Study* (Nashville: Publishing House of the M. E. Church, South, 1909), p. 45.

[28] Tipple, *Francis Asbury*, p. 105; Herbert Asbury, *Methodist Saint*, p. 283.

In examining the arrangement, you will find every particular head well furnished with suitable hymns, in which are contained a body of excellent divinity, explanatory of, and enforcing the fundamental doctrines of the Gospel. We now cheerfully commend the work and you to the protection and care of Almighty God, hoping you will still sing with the Spirit and understanding also; guarding particularly against lifeless formality in this and all other devotional exercises, till you are called to join the innumerable company who in heaven sing the song of Moses and of the lamb.[29]

In the interest of unity and peace in the church, he extracted parts from *Heart Divisions, The Evil of Our Times* by Jeremiah Burroughs and *The Cure of Church Divisions* by Richard Baxter. These extracts he published together under the title *The Causes, Evils, and Cures of Heart and Church Divisions*. This editing job evidently got some readers. Its preface commended it widely, not only to bickering Methodists but to all Christians; James O'Kelly took the trouble to rebut it in chapter 33 of his *Apology*, and the book was reprinted as late as 1849.[30]

When the *Arminian Magazine* had failed after two years and its successor *The Methodist Magazine* had lasted just as long, Asbury still wanted to spread the word about revival as that news came to him. Therefore, he edited some revival reports from his presiding elders and published them in 1805 as *Extracts of Letters, Containing Some Account of the Work of God Since the Year 1800*.

Last night, about eleven o'clock, we closed our annual meeting; and, glory to God, he has done wonders. About one hundred and thirteen white and black were joined in society yesterday; and from what I hear, I doubt not, but as many, if not twice the number, who went away wounded and crippled, sick and sore, will be joined in different parts of the country—all the fruits of this blessed meeting.[31]

[29] (New York: Wilson and Hitt, 1808), p. iv.

[30] *The Causes, Evils, and Cures of Heart and Church Divisions* (New York: Lane and Scott, 1849); JLFA, III, 45-46.

[31] Extract from Richard Bassett, p. 19.

After reading a hundred pages of these, a Methodist preacher who could not produce a revival would want to shoot himself.

It was Asbury's *Journal* the Book Concern wanted. This was his pride and joy. He intended it to be his only biography and the best history of Methodism for the years of his life. It would tell the true facts of every controversy and vindicate him wholly. Out of love for the *Arminian Magazine* he allowed some extracts from his *Journal* to be published there in 1789. Though he intended the *Journal* for publication, he was reluctant to allow it to be published in his lifetime. He himself cleansed it of some marginal and polemic material. Then he enlisted a series of editors to make it fit and ready for the press.

> I was presented with a new impression of my journal; it is very incorrect: had I had an opportunity before it was put to press, I should have altered and expunged many things; the inaccuracies of grammar, and imperfections of composition incident to the hasty notices of a manuscript journal are preserved in the printed copy.[32]

> I sit seven hours a day, looking over and hearing read my transcribed journal: we have examined and approved up to 1807. As a record of the early history of Methodism in America, my journal will be of use; and accompanied by the minutes of the conferences, will tell all that will be necessary to know. I have buried in shades all that will be proper to forget, in which I am personally concerned; if truth and I have been wronged, we have both witnessed our day of triumph.[33]

> Joseph Lanston, and myself have concluded he shall devote his time to finish the transcription of my journal. I wish a number or two at a time may be sent to Doctor Wilkins to correct and abridge, because only the most interesting parts will be preserved.[34]

The first full edition of Asbury's *Journal* dates from 1821.[35]

[32] April 5, 1802; JLFA, II, 332-33.
[33] June 29, 1815; JLFA, II, 783.
[34] To Mrs. Ann Willis, August 29, 1813; JLFA, III, 494.
[35] See JLFA, I, xv-xviii.

If Asbury was not able to prepare the bulk of the books for American Methodists himself, he could certainly arrange for others to do it. There was all the literary wealth of Wesley and of English Methodism to be imported. Certainly the pioneer Methodists had carried some Wesleyan literature to America with them. The accounts of John Street Church in New York indicate that Philip Embury and Joseph Pilmoor sold some books and turned the money over to the church in 1770.[36] Asbury himself seems to have carried some copies of Fletcher's *Checks* to stop the mouths of those he suspected as antinomians.[37] Methodist preacher Robert Williams began reprinting and selling Wesley's sermons without authorization. Asbury accused him of selling some of them for personal profit, which "does by no means look well." By action of the first American conference in 1773 such reprinting without permission was forbidden; Williams could sell what he had but print no more. The American Methodists must have books, but an enterprise so vital must be rightly ordered.

Asbury had a large share in getting out the books for Methodist education. Between 1773 and 1782 a plan was developed to publish and sell books, using the profits to help pay expenses of traveling preachers. This was approved by the conferences in 1782. Each itinerant and local preacher was to deal in books; he was to beg money from the rich and buy books for the poor. In 1789 John Dickins was appointed as "book steward," and he published 114,000 books and tracts before his death in the yellow fever epidemic of 1798.[38] Then Asbury appointed Ezekiel Cooper to head the "Book Concern," as he had called it in his *Journal* as far back as April 26, 1786. Cooper at first was hard put to keep the work going, but had the satisfaction of reporting book concern assets of $45,000 when he retired in 1808. In spite of many stormy days, the Book Concern was a most valued part of American Methodism from the time of Dickins. It was by far the first among American

[36] J. B. Wakeley, *Lost Chapters Recovered from the Early History of American Methodism* (New York: Carlton and Porter, 1858), pp. 105-7.

[37] June 28, 1773, and August 15, 1774; JLFA, I, 83, 128.

[38] William Warren Sweet, *Religion on the American Frontier, 1783-1840, Vol. IV: The Methodists* (Chicago: University of Chicago Press, 1946), p. 680.

denominational publishing houses and the source of the only cash some Methodist preachers ever saw.[39]

No matter who headed the Book Concern, Francis Asbury worked in it too. Its financial health was a matter of life or death to his preachers. The books and leaflets were, next to preaching, his best hope for reaching his preachers and people. Even such a critic of formal learning as Peter Cartwright could look back over his long ministry and say in his *Autobiography* in 1856:

> It has often been a question that I shall never be able to answer on earth, whether I have done the most good by preaching or distributing religious books. If we as a Church had been blessed with a flourishing Book Concern such as we now have, and our preachers had scattered books broad-cast over these Western wilds, or any other wilds, it would be impossible to tell the vast amount of good that would have been done. And, indeed, this is one of the grand secrets of the success of our early Methodist preachers.[40]

Asbury's church structure became a sales organization for Methodist literature. By the General Conference of 1800 the plan was carefully described:

> It shall be the duty of every presiding elder, where no book-steward is appointed, to see that his district be duly supplied with books: he is to request the superintendent to send such books as are wanted, and give direction to whose care the same are to be sent; and he is to take the oversight of all the books sent to his district, and to account with the superintendent for the same: he is to have the books distributed among the several circuits in his district, in such quantities and in such a manner as he may judge proper from his own information, and keep an account with each preacher, who receives and sells the books: he is to receive the money and forward it to the superintendent. . . .
>
> The preachers shall be allowed for their trouble not less than fifteen, nor more than twenty-five per cent., upon the wholesale price

[39] See HAM, I, 281-87.
[40] P. 187.

for all the books they sell; but the per cent. shall be regulated as in the judgment of the superintendent the different impressions will afford, one-third of which the presiding elder shall have for his trouble, and the other two-thirds shall be allowed to the preachers who sell them in their different circuits.[41]

Thus as Asbury made his rounds among his presiding elders he also settled the accounts and transacted the business of the Book Concern. This was often delegated to one of his traveling companions in later years. When Asbury himself became so weak and sick that he could not preach to everyone he met on his rounds, he personally carried a supply of tracts in German and English to give or sell, and so do as much good as he could.[42] When he died he gave his small fortune to the Book Concern, and through it to the poor preachers and their dependents.

Asbury knew his preachers were not educated; he meant for them to study.

A taste for reading profitable books is an inestimable gift. It adds to the comfort of life far beyond what many conceive, and qualifies us, if properly directed, for very extensive usefulness in the church of God. It takes off all the miserable listlessness of a sluggish life; and gives to the mind a strength and activity it could not otherwise acquire. But to obtain and preserve this taste for, this delight in, profitable reading, we must daily resist the natural tendency of man to indolence and idleness.[43]

The *Discipline* of 1785 admonished preachers to "read the most useful Books, and that regularly and constantly." They were under instruction to "spend all the Morning in this Employment, or at least five hours in four and twenty." There is no reason to think very many of them actually did it. No systematic check was made. No course of reading and study was even formulated until General Conference of 1816, the year Asbury died.

[41] *Journals of the General Conference . . . 1796-1836*, pp. 45, 46.
[42] Smith, *Life of Francis Asbury*, p. 263.
[43] *Discipline*, 1798, p. 107.

Asbury wanted all the people to have the rudiments of education, "the key of knowledge in a general way." But in fact, the literary level of most of his constituents was very low and fast getting lower as the population poured into the great west. None of his schemes for schools came to life in spite of his pains as a planner and as a reluctant fund raiser. What he did was to get out the books and keep bearing testimony against mere ignorance. His was a kind of holding action in education until the next generation, when some combination of tradition and curiosity and shame was to make Methodism a great founder of schools.

11
PILGRIM

Francis Asbury was not a many-sided man; he was a one-sided man. He was unabashedly religious. The interests of his religion he identified squarely with the interests of God. If he was not one hundred percent religious, it was not because he did not intend to be. If all other Americans were not one hundred percent religious, that was but an indication of the work which he must do. He moved from the religious intensity of his home into the religious intensity of Wesleyan Methodism without a sign of rebellion. They were willing steps on his chosen way.

The world was not to be despised, for God made it. Human beings were not to be despised, because Christ died for them. Asbury knew people in tens and scores and thousands. He genuinely loved people—as individuals and in mass. But it was always their deepest selves, their souls, he wanted. Polite company and worldly conversation were tolerable at best; it was more important to keep oneself unspotted from such trappings.

Was confined in the evening to the company of men who were destitute of religion, and full of sin and politics. My brethren and myself

were glad to have prayer in the morning and leave them. If there
were no other hell than the company of wicked men, I would say,
From such a hell, good Lord, deliver me! [1]

Said a contemporary who knew him well:

To all that bore the appearance of polished and pleasing life he was
dead; . . . he seemed to estimate nothing as excellent but what tended
to the glory of God. . . . He was a rigid enemy to ease; hence, the
pleasures of study and the charms of recreation, he alike sacrificed to
the more sublime work of saving souls. His faith was a "constant
evidence of things not seen," for he lived as a man totally blind to
all worldly attractions. . . . Although . . . in his company upon a
variety of occasions, I never saw him indulge in even innocent pleas-
antry: his was the solemnity of an Apostle; it was so interwoven
with his conduct, that he could not put off the gravity of the Bishop,
either in the parlor or dining-room. [2]

He was always impatient to get to ultimate questions with
every man. Diversions were only diverting. Biographers do no
service by trying to normalize Asbury with a few doubtful cita-
tions of his humor or his social sparkle or his unbending with
children or his love for his horses. When he sat for a portrait
or planned a vacation it was so out of character that the reader is
as uncomfortable as Asbury until the thing is over. James
McCannon did get him to sit for a portrait once by promising
that if Asbury would sit, he, McCannon, would make a velvet
vest for each of Asbury's preachers. [3] For a charity so grand even
he might compromise a little with the world.

When he went to Hot Springs it was to take the baths; between
baths there was not loafing but preaching. [4] He turned aside to see
a test of a primitive steamboat and pronounced it "a great inven-
tion." [5] But one suspects he had some vision of the expansion of

[1] May 8, 1775; JLFA, I, 156.

[2] Marsden, *Poems on Methodism*, pp. 104-5.

[3] George C. Roberts, *Centenary Pictorial Album* (Baltimore: J. W. Woods, 1866),
pp. 16-17.

[4] August, 1787; JLFA, I, 548-49.

[5] May 1, 1809; JLFA, II, 601.

Methodism by steamboat; he was not the type to be wondering where he could lay hands on some cash to buy stock in the company. He wanted none of the trivia of humans; it was their salvation he was after. It appears that the fact of his own dead seriousness allowed people to be serious with him. They knew who he was and where he stood without having to do a lot of psychological sparring.

Heaven was his home and goal. For this brief earthly expedition, voluntary discipline was most fitting. One must give no offense or cause for stumbling to the weak; one must make every hour count; one must give glory to God and bring men to salvation. So he studied under discipline.

> My present mode of conduct is as follows—to read about a hundred pages a day; usually to pray in public five times a day; to preach in the open air every other day; to lecture in prayer meeting every evening. And if it were in my power, I would do a thousand times as much for such a gracious and blessed Master.[6]

American roads and trails were so bad that he complained he could not read on horseback "as Mr. Wesley does in England."[7] He could at least review his grammar while riding. "I have been employed in improving myself in the Hebrew tones and points; this being my horseback study."[8]

Most of his study was done before the day's journey began and before retirement at night. Generally he rose very early in the morning and studied until it was time for breakfast or morning worship. In the evening he tried to study at least one hour more.

> Arose before three. I am much employed, but it is good to make the best of every moment, and carefully to fill up the space of time that may be lost. O! how precious is time! Our moments, though little, are golden sands.[9]

[6] July 29, 1776; JLFA, I, 195.
[7] September 11, 1781; JLFA, I, 411.
[8] March 6, 1793; JLFA, I, 750.
[9] July 27, 1779; JLFA, I, 307.

I purposed to rise at four o'clock, as often as I can, and spend two hours in prayer and meditation; two hours in reading, and one in recreating and conversation; and in the evening, to take my room at eight, pray and meditate an hour, and go to bed at nine o'clock: all this I purpose to do, when not travelling; but to rise at four o'clock every morning.[10]

This morning, I ended the reading my Bible through, in about four months. It is hard work for me to find time for this; but all I read and write, I owe to early rising. If I were not to rise always by five, and sometimes at four o'clock, I should have no time only to eat my breakfast, pray in the family, and get ready for my journey—as I must travel every day.[11]

He knew the New Testament nearly by memory. But he was always working on something besides the Bible as well; the list of his reading is amazing. There were biographies, history tomes, controversial works of theology, sermons by great preachers, and mounds of devotional literature which would deepen all the more his pilgrim motivations. "I spent much of my time in reading Law's Serious Call and Baxter's Call to the Unconverted; and think the latter is one of the best pieces of human composition in the world, to awaken the lethargic souls of poor sinners." [12]

Along with his reading he prayed. The devil is always willing to have us read if we will not pray, said he.[13]

Whenever he stopped for the night he prayed; wherever he ate he closed the meal with prayer. At the approach of Conference he sought opportunities of special prayer for divine guidance. At one time it was his practice to set apart three hours of every twenty-four for this spiritual exercise; at another period in his life he gave himself to private prayer seven times a day; at another time it was his habit to spend a part of every hour when awake praying; at still another, ten minutes of every hour.[14]

[10] November 17, 1779; JLFA, I, 323.
[11] August 26, 1779; JLFA, I, 311.
[12] September 3, 1777; JLFA, I, 248.
[13] September 20, 1779; JLFA, I, 314.
[14] Tipple, *Francis Asbury*, p. 308.

Once he resolved he would pray for every Methodist preacher every day, but as the church grew, that project got out of hand. The plan for prayer shifted and modified. There is no clue that the priority of prayer was ever displaced or that his faithful practice of it ever wavered. "Every family shall know me by prayer" was his expressed intention.

He also fasted. The urgency for this practice among Methodists had come over into the first *Discipline* almost verbatim from the Large Minutes of 1780 from England.

Question 52. Why are not *we* more holy? . . .

Answer   Chiefly because we are Enthusiasts; look for the End without using the Means. . . . Do you know the Obligation and the Benefit of *Fasting?* How often do you practise it?

Question 53. But how can I fast since it hurts my Health?

Answer   There are several Degrees of Fasting, which can not hurt your Health. We will instance in one. Let us every Friday (beginning on the next) avow this Duty throughout the Continent, by touching no Tea, Coffee or Chocolate *in the Morning,* but (if we want it) half a Pint of Milk or Water-Gruel. Let us dine on Vegetables, and (if we need it) eat three or four Ounces of Flesh in the evening.[15]

It is plain from repeated references in the *Journal* that Asbury regularly fasted at least to this degree, and perhaps more strenuously. Many times the entry is very straightforward for a Friday.

Friday, 19. I kept a day of fasting and humiliation.[16]

Friday, 13. . . . I fasted from yesterday noon until four o'clock to-day; though much tempted, I have been blest.[17]

[15] *Discipline*, 1785, pp. 17-18.
[16] November 19, 1779; JLFA, I, 323.
[17] July 13, 1781; JLFA, I, 408.

Friday, 7. . . . This was a day of fasting: I ate nothing till after three o'clock, and then only a bowl of milk; amidst all my exercises, I feel as though I advanced in the Divine life; am thankful that I am so well provided for, when, no doubt, thousands are suffering the want of food, firing, house room, and clothing. O! may I act worthy of these favours! [18]

When fasting dropped out of usage among the American Methodists, there was a plea from the General Conference of 1812.

The important duty of *fasting* has almost become obsolete. This we are afraid will be productive of melancholy effects. We yet have abundant cause for deep humiliation before God and one another. Our country is threatened, calamities stare us in the face, iniquity abounds, and the love of many waxes cold. O let us again resort to fasting and humiliation.[19]

Whether or not the voice of the conference was the voice of Asbury, the advice accorded with his own feeling and practice even in his old age.

I wish to fast as when young, and when fast day comes, the body has a journey of forty miles to make, perhaps, and do its part of preaching: but Christ is strength in my weakness.[20]

Oh, that you would seek the Lord by fasting or abstinance every week to do away all the disagreeables from your mind, and every bar to usefulness! [21]

Single-mindedness in religion made Asbury effective. No zeal for America or for Methodism or for personal power would be enough to explain his life and work without this religious drive. His *Journal* and his biographers bear unanimous witness of the marvelous motivating purpose. He was engaged in a work of God

[18] January 7, 1780; JLFA, I, 330.
[19] Bangs, *History of the M. E. Church,* II, 329.
[20] July 9, 1809; JLFA, II, 608.
[21] To Thomas Haskins, April 21, 1809; *Methodist History,* April, 1964, p. 60.

which dare not be denied. The power he wanted was not for himself but for his mission. That mission was clear: all America was to be won to saving confession of Jesus Christ as Savior and then to produce the fruits of holiness. There must be no delay. Everything else was less important than souls.

To an amazing degree, Asbury was able to communicate his zeal for the goal and his plan for reaching it. Perhaps the evangelical understanding of man's plight and the evangelical understanding of the means to salvation were so uniform among the rank and file at the end of the eighteenth century that he had a common ground with many before he said a word. But Asbury himself was an important catalyst. In his episcopal function he combined elements of the martyr, of the military commander, and of the evangelist. One biographer makes an undocumented claim that Asbury hoped to receive the stigmata in his flesh like Francis of Assisi.[22] If he did not generate the vital force of Methodism, at least he channeled it to such a multiplication of ministry and such a unity of membership and method as to put a stamp on the whole history of America.

It is obvious that power combined with such certainty and single-mindedness may lead to tyranny. If one equates his mission fully with God's plan, how shall he tolerate opposition? If he is resisted, is not God resisted? Asbury's critics have accused him of such fallacy. Pilmoor complained of the bossiness of young Asbury. Coke found that although he was senior bishop and presiding officer, he was always steered in his American work by Asbury. James O'Kelly made his main theme the tyranny or popery of Asbury; O'Kelly's eccentricity has usually been enough to discredit his charges. Asbury's friends also noted the autocratic tendency. Devereux Jarratt spoke of "his strong passion for superiority and thirst for domination." [23] In the midst of the eulogy at Asbury's funeral, Ezekiel Cooper conceded that the bishop was more deficient in the exercise of patience than in any

[22] Herbert Asbury, *Methodist Saint*, p. 264.
[23] Tipple, *Francis Asbury*, p. 323.

of the Christian graces.[24] Nicholas Snethen, who traveled with Asbury, said:

> It cannot be concealed, that he was not incapable of the exercise of that awful attribute of power, hardheartedness to those individual personal feelings and interests, which seem to oppose the execution of public plans. Constantly in the habit of making the greatest personal sacrifices to the public good, his mind could not balance betwixt the obligation of duty, and the accommodation, or conveniency of others.[25]

Even prayer could be used as a weapon against dissenters. Ira Ellis relates that Asbury was listening to some preachers complain about their poor support and their hard work. Asbury called them to prayer:

> Lord, we are in thy hands and in thy work. Thou knowest what is best for us and for thy work, whether poverty or plenty. The hearts of all men are in thy hands. If it is best for us and for thy Church that we should be cramped and straitened, let the people's hands and hearts be closed. If it is better for us—for the Church— and more to thy glory that we should abound in the comforts of life, do thou dispose the hearts of those we serve to give accordingly; and may we learn to be content, whether we abound or suffer need.[26]

The dissension died.

Perhaps the only thing which saved Asbury from ruthless autocracy was the same religious faith which inspired and motivated him. Never for long was he free from a sense of his own unworthiness. Even when he felt sure of his saving allegiance to Christ, his longing for more holiness was so great that he was always the seeker. His *Journal* entries are an endless chain of introspections. He was always taking his spiritual temperature or stretching out his soul under the glass. Sometimes there was ground for hope.

[24] *Substance of a Funeral Discourse* (Philadelphia: Jonathan Pounder, 1819), p. 179.
[25] "A Discourse on the Death of the Reverend Francis Asbury," in Feeman, *Francis Asbury's Silver Trumpet*, p. 131.
[26] Tipple, *Francis Asbury*, p. 326.

My general experience is close communion with God, holy fellowship with the Father and his Son Jesus Christ, a will resigned, frequent addresses to a throne of grace, a constant, serious care for the prosperity of Zion, forethought in the arrangements and appointments of the preachers, a soul drawn out in ardent prayer for the universal Church and the complete triumph of Christ over the whole earth.[27]

On *Friday* the Lord graciously blessed me with sweet peace, and much love.[28]

My body is in a feeble state; but glory to God, when I am weak, then am I strong. Though this mortal frame is shaken by repeated afflictions, my soul is supported by that peace which passeth all understanding.[29]

O Lord, help me to watch and pray! I am afraid of losing the sweetness I feel: for months past I have felt as if in the possession of perfect love; not a moment's desire of anything but God.[30]

Quite as often he was depressed.

I do not sufficiently love God, nor live by faith in the suburbs of heaven.[31]

My body is weak; but this does not concern me like the want of more grace. My heart is too cool towards God: I want to feel it like a holy flame.[32]

For my unholiness and unfaithfulness, my soul is humbled: were I to stand on my own merit, where should I be or go, but to hell? [33]

He was very severe in judging himself for failures in discipline. Since William Law thought people slept too much, and John Wes-

[27] December 28, 1802; JLFA, II, 372.
[28] December 23, 1773; JLFA, I, 99.
[29] February 9, 1779; JLFA, I, 295.
[30] September 28, 1791; JLFA, I, 696.
[31] October 28, 1774; JLFA, I, 136.
[32] August 19, 1775; JLFA, I, 162.
[33] March 2, 1796; JLFA, II, 79.

ley thought six hours of sleep enough for any man, Asbury reproached himself for any indulgence.

I felt some conviction for sleeping too long.[34]

Unguarded and trifling conversation has brought on a degree of spiritual deadness.[35]

My conscience smote me severely for speaking an idle word in company. O! how frail is man. It is very difficult for me to check my rapid flow of spirits when in company with my friends.[36]

I reproved myself for a sudden and violent laugh at the relation of a man's having given an old Negro woman her liberty *because she had too much religion for him.*[37]

The "assaults of Satan" were repeated and awful. These struggles often brought him to the very brink of despair.

The next day some of my friends were so unguarded and imprudent as to commend me to my face. Satan, ready for every advantage, seized the opportunity and assaulted me with self-pleasing, self-exalting ideas. But the Lord enabled me to discover the danger, and the snare was broken. May he ever keep me humble, and little, and mean, in my own eyes! [38]

I have lately been grievously haunted by the temptations of Satan; but my desire is to die rather than live to sin against God. Lord, stand by me in the day of trial, and every moment support my feeble soul! On Saturday also my mind was much harassed by my spiritual adversary; and my study and devotion were interrupted, so that I could do but little either for God or myself.[39]

Satan beset me with powerful suggestions, striving to persuade me that I should never conquer all my spiritual enemies, but be over-

---

[34] August 15, 1774; JLFA, I, 128.
[35] November 18, 1774; JLFA, I, 138.
[36] February 1, 1779; JLFA, I, 295.
[37] November 4, 1790; JLFA, I, 655-56.
[38] May 13, 1774; JLFA, I, 115.
[39] May 1, 1778; JLFA, I, 269.

come at last. However, the Lord was near, and filled my soul with peace. Blessed Lord, be ever with me, and suffer me not to yield to the tempter; no, not for a moment! [40]

His best hope for overcoming the depression was activity. When he was out of the episcopal harness, all his potential for anguish came to the fore, and the assaults were nearly unbearable.

Blessed are ye when men shall say all manner of evil of you falsely for my sake, saith the Lord. O, how ought I to be humbled, that such trifles affect me! But I speculate too much, and reason upon the dark side.[41]

I have my trials, and believe it is because I am not so extensively in the work as I hope to be shortly.[42]

I find my greatest trials to arise from "taking thought:" it is by this Satan trys to come in: it is my constitutional weakness to be gloomy and dejected; the work of God puts life into me—and why despond? the land is before us, and nothing can hurt us but divisions among ourselves.[43]

In his later years he preached the need for holiness more and more. Sanctification was to be his theme in every sermon. But he never claimed himself to have arrived at perfection. The old traveler was a bishop and a commander and a martyr, but he remained a seeker. He was not yet an archangel; he was only bound for the heavenly land.

---

[40] April 29, 1776; JLFA, I, 185.
[41] August 29, 1779; JLFA, I, 311.
[42] January 5, 1780; JLFA, I, 330.
[43] February 24, 1782; JLFA, I, 421-22.

PART III

The Cardinal Points

12
EVANGELISM

To be converted, to be regenerated, to receive grace, to experience religion, to gain an assurance, are so many phrases which denote the process, gradual or sudden, by which a self hitherto divided, and consciously wrong inferior and unhappy, becomes unified and consciously right superior and happy, in consequence of its firmer hold upon religious realities.[1]

So William James said it in his Gifford Lectures 100 years after the time of Asbury. And 150 years after Asbury, Erwin Goodenough of Yale says out of his maturity:

But all branches of Christianity have insisted that by this grace men are definitely improved during their lifetime over what they would be without it.

This is the old doctrine, and let us be fair about it. If we do not believe in the grace of Christ and his salvation as things with historical and metaphysical existence, we cannot deny that millions

[1] William James, *The Varieties of Religious Experience* (New York: Collier, 1961), p. 160.

through the ages have been "saved"—that is enormously improved —by believing just that about Christ, and by "accepting" his grace. To doubt this is not scientific reserve, but the capital crime of the scientific age, prejudiced refusal to believe a fact.[2]

Asbury would hardly have understood their caution. He gave most of his life to the enterprise of evangelism wrought by conversion under revival preaching, and he understood it much as Wesley did.[3] There might be enemies of such evangelism, but what was new about there being enemies of God? There might be resisters of such evangelism, but Satan could not be expected to give up easily. There might be men who were spiritually dead, but they were the very ones who needed to be wakened with the word of the gospel as the Methodists preached it.

Wesley understood conversion as he had experienced it at Aldersgate, as he read about it in Jonathan Edwards' *Faithful Narrative,* and as he saw it happening, to his amazement, under his own preaching at Bristol.[4] Later he illustrated proper evangelism with his figure of the house. A man came under conviction because of his depravity and sin; this was to stand on the porch facing the house of salvation. A man heard the word, repented, knew the wonderful release from the burden of his sin and was justified; this was to attain the threshold of the house of salvation. But the threshold attained by conversion was no place to stop. The Christian must now move on to what was variously called holiness, perfection, second justification, or sanctification. This was a kind of consummation of Christian maturity which might be arrived at after growth in the Christian life and was to be followed by more Christian growth. To be possessed by this mature purity of devotion and love toward God and man, this was to enter the very house of salvation.[5]

---

[2] Erwin R. Goodenough, *Toward a Mature Faith* (New York: Prentice-Hall, 1955), p. 138.

[3] See Sydney G. Dimond, *The Psychology of the Methodist Revival* (Nashville: Whitmore and Smith, 1926), pp. 158-68.

[4] Outler, *John Wesley,* pp. 15-17.

[5] To Thomas Church, June 17, 1746; LJW, II, 268-70.

Asbury, at every point of his understanding of salvation, was a Wesleyan just one shade less restrained. Wesley developed his ideal for Christian performance from reading Jeremy Taylor, Thomas à Kempis, and William Law.[6] Asbury read them all over again and was equally impressed: "I afterward returned safe to town in the evening; and spent a part of the next day in reading Taylor's Treatise on Holy Living. This book was made a blessing to me above seven years ago." [7] Wesley wanted his hearers not only to think but to feel. Good preaching was the kind which made the very words *feelable*. Following his own experience and the witness of those impressive conversions under his field preaching at Bristol, he expected his hearers to be visibly affected and their lives to be transformed. Asbury was direct heir of all this. He had been movingly converted as a boy. From the beginning of his service in America he expected his preaching to stir intense feeling in the hearers.

Early in the morning we crossed the North river, in order to go to Staten Island. Many people attended the word; but I know not what to make of them; for though they seem fond of hearing, yet they do not appear to be much affected.[8]

At present a spirit of harmony subsisteth amongst our leaders [in New York]; but I want to see them also deeply engaged to take the kingdom of heaven by violence.[9]

Conversion was man's business as Asbury saw it. God had arranged for it all; His grace was prevenient and moving and melting. The life and death and resurrection of Jesus Christ had now given the enabling grace to all men. So men must now hear the

---

[6] Outler, *John Wesley*, p. 79; John L. Peters, *Christian Perfection and American Methodism* (Nashville: Abingdon Press, 1956), p. 19.

[7] March 18, 1775; JLFA, I, 152.

[8] August 24, 1772; JLFA, I, 40.

[9] November 3, 1774; JLFA, I, 137.

gospel and be moved to exercise the grace which God had given them. Men, being depraved, were not easy to move, but moved they must be. Salvation was something one went out for; conversion was to be wrought.

> A fine, sensible, polite gentleman delivered a discourse on the new birth; he described it by its effects, but appeared to be at a total loss in respect to the manner in which it is wrought. I had spoken in the morning, and in the evening preached again, pressing religion on the young people especially, and showing the superior advantages and satisfaction arising from it even in this life.[10]

> Little sleep last night. Let me suffer, and let me labour; time is short, and souls are daily lost.[11]

Asbury and his preachers solemnly put the call of life or death. They could be terrifying. "I preached some awful truths," said Asbury.[12] "Take heed, brethren, lest there be in any of you an evil heart of unbelief," they said.[13] Or, "The wages of sin is death; but the gift of God is eternal life." [14] The very love of God put the hearer under compulsion to leave his old way and seek salvation. Bishops Coke and Asbury charged the preacher to

> Convince the sinner of his dangerous condition. . . . He must set forth the depth of original sin, and shew the sinner how far he is gone from original righteousness; he must describe the vices of the world in their just and most striking colours, and enter into all the sinner's pleas and excuses for sin, and drive him from all his subterfuges and strongholds.[15]

Those who came "under conviction" were often in great heaviness and personal distress, but, noisy or quiet, they were on the porch of salvation.

[10] August 11, 1776; JLFA, I, 196.
[11] February 16, 1812; JLFA, II, 694.
[12] March 1, 1812; JLFA, II, 694.
[13] Heb. 3:12, April 12, 1794; JLFA, II, 12.
[14] Rom. 6:23, October 17, 1779; JLFA, I, 317.
[15] Discipline, 1798, p. 86.

One by one they crossed the threshold of conversion. The preacher could not stop at convincing the sinner of his "dangerous condition" but must go on to "bring the mourner to a *present* Saviour: he must show the willingness of Christ *this moment* to bless him, and bring a present salvation *home* to his soul." [16] The crossing was usually tumultuous. Some were physically struck down, only to rise up a little later singing, leaping, and praying in thankfulness. Some suffered through days, weeks, and months of misery to rival the awful wrestling of Whitefield. When the release came, with its surety of forgiveness and justification,

> this was the "glorious liberty" of the children of God! And this was worth shouting about, for it affected both time and eternity!
> And shout they did! The Methodist meetings often were characterized by the climactic outcries of those seeking—and finding—some deeply personal assurance of the Divine mercy.[17]

> We met people coming from the militia muster, drunk, and staggering along the lanes and paths; these unhappy souls have had their camp meeting and shout forth the praises of the god of strong drink: glory be to God, we have our camp meetings too; of longer continuance, and more and louder shouting of glory, and honour, and praises to the God of the armies of the earth. Go on, ye servants of the Lord; and Thou, mighty Saviour, extend the victories of Gospel grace! [18]

> The work of God is wonderful in Delaware. But what a *rumpus* is raised! We are subverters of government—disturbers of society—movers of insurrections. Grand juries in Delaware and Virginia have presented the noisy preachers—lawyers and doctors are in arms—the lives, blood, and livers of the poor Methodists are threatened: poor, crazy sinners! see ye not that the Lord is with us? [19]

Even Coke wrote, "All the shouting seasons, in spite of my proud reluctance to yield to them at first, were a matter of great

[16] *Ibid.*
[17] Leland Scott, "The Message of Early American Methodism," HAM, I, 299.
[18] November 5, 1803; JLFA, II, 413.
[19] December 25, 1806; JLFA, II, 524.

praise and rejoicing to me very soon: and I shall defend them, both from the pulpit and the press, throughout the European part of our connection." [20]

Each preacher told and retold the story of his own conversion. Each recipient of assurance told of his experience in the class meeting or the love feast. If he lost his assurance and backslid, he often sought the prayers of his brethren to come to a new experience; then at the meetings he narrated both. This lively preaching and singing and experience and testimony brought great crowds to Methodist meetings, crowds full of expectancy. They in turn were convicted and converted so that some whole families and neighborhoods and settlements were enrolled. Asbury could say in Virginia, "A hundred souls have been brought to God: thus the barren wilderness begins to smile." [21] And in Maryland: "It seems as if the whole Peninsula must be *methodised*." [22] And in Ohio: "The Methodists seem to have almost entire influence in this town." [23] Some other observers were saying, "At this rate the Methodists will get all the people." This very success was to be the ground for Asbury's urgency to preach sanctification.

Once again the doctrine was Wesley's. Wholly at one with the Protestant Reformers, Wesley affirmed God's remarkable seeking grace toward man and his free gift of redemption to those who respond. Both God's searching grace and man's faithful response are focused in Jesus Christ, the very Word of God become man. This is justification: God sees every man who will earnestly receive his grace and respond to it as savingly one with Jesus Christ, who is the elder brother, the new head, the embodiment of all the redeemed. So justification is an immediate cosmic act, and God does it. "I think on Justification just as I have done any time these seven-and-twenty years, and just as Mr. Calvin does. In this respect I do not differ from him an hair's breadth." [24]

Wesley and the Calvinists could also agree that the believer, the

[20] To Freeborn Garrettson, July 6, 1789; HAM, I, 300.
[21] January 16, 1790; JLFA, I, 621.
[22] April 23, 1803; JLFA, II, 388.
[23] September 15, 1812; JLFA, II, 708.
[24] To John Newton, May 14, 1765; LJW, IV, 298.

man justified in God's sight, was to seek sanctification. Sanctification is the dying to sin and coming alive to righteousness which mark a mature Christian. Calvinists viewed sanctification as a long uphill pull toward holiness which followed the profession of faithful response; for the faithful the gracious progression of sanctification was crowned with the gift of perfection at death. Wesley believed that Christians must grow as long as they live, but in view of his theology of evangelism and in view of some individual experiences he reached a different conclusion. He used the terms perfection, holiness, and sanctification as synonyms to designate a new state based on an instantaneous act of faith in some Christians, and he believed he knew some Christians who had reached it. In fact, it was the preacher's duty to urge all believers on to perfection here and now. They should expect to attain it, and not be content without it. Wesley marshaled his scripture texts and his human examples. He kept explaining that he did not mean any Christian was ever spared from infirmity, ignorance, or mistake. He issued an appalling list of warnings to those who might think they had attained perfection too easily. But he still insisted on a Christian perfection attainable in this life which preachers should lift up before their people.

1. By perfection I mean the humble, gentle, patient love of God and our neighbour, ruling our tempers, words, and actions.

I do not include an impossibility of falling from it, either in part or in whole. Therefore, I retract several expressions in our hymns, which partly express, partly imply, such an impossibility.

And I do not contend for the term *sinless*, though I do not object against it.

2. As to the manner. I believe this perfection is always wrought in the soul by a simple act of faith; consequently in an instant. But I believe in a gradual work both preceding and following that instant.

3. As to time. I believe this instant generally is the instant of death, the moment before the soul leaves the body. But I believe it may be ten, twenty, or forty years before.[25]

[25] Wesley, *A Plain Account of Christian Perfection* (London: Epworth, 1952), pp. 112, 33, 35-37, 42, 62-69, 86-97.

Asbury probably preached this because he believed it and because it was Wesleyan; the two motivations are hardly separable in him. But the tremendous drive for the preaching of perfection came out of his American setting. Here was a land with a very large rural population of unchurched or nominally churched people. Under the highly electric ministry of the Methodist revival thousands upon thousands of them crossed the threshold of justification by conversion. As they saw it, they were saved. Asbury immediately saw the problem of maintaining religious growth and intensity in such a mass of converts. "Such is the languid disposition of the human soul, that even pure minds require a constant stimulation to keep them in the way of duty." [26]

There was always his preaching on the dangers of backsliding. At the very time cited when one hundred were converted and "the barren wilderness begins to smile," he added: "I found it a time to speak from Isaiah lii, 1." [27] The text reads "Awake, awake; put on thy strength, O Zion; put on thy beautiful garments, O Jerusalem, the holy city: for henceforth there shall no more come into thee the uncircumcised and the unclean." His outline from the text II Peter 2:20-21 stated that real Christians had escaped from the pollutions of the world, but it was possible for them to be entangled therein again and overcome. Then, "the last state of such is worse than the first: for God is provoked, Christ slighted, the Spirit grieved, religion dishonoured, their understanding is darkened, the will is perverted, the conscience becomes insensible, and all the affections unmoved under the means of grace." [28] He had an arsenal of sermons for backsliders, and one suspects that this theme entered most every sermon whatever the text.

But he came to believe there was an even better way than preaching against backsliding. That was to preach for Christian perfection. As he grew older and the Methodist Episcopal Church grew larger, he focused more and more on the quest for perfection.

[26] October 7, 1777; JLFA, I, 250.
[27] January 16, 1790; JLFA, I, 621.
[28] July 4, 1794; JLFA, II, 19.

My soul was in peace; but I have not sufficiently enforced the doctrine of Christian perfection. This will press believers forward, when everything else is found insufficient; and the people in these parts appear ripe for it—for there is little or no opposition.[29]

Blessed be God, I enjoy good health of body and peace of mind! I find no preaching does good, but that which properly presses the use of the means, and urges holiness of heart; these points I am determined to keep close to in all my sermons.[30]

I am filled with love from day to day. O bless the Lord for the constant communion I enjoy with him! Sanctification is the doctrine which is most wanted to be preached among the people here, whom the more I know the more I love: Antinomians are labouring to spread their tenets among them; but they will give way, as holiness of heart and life is pointedly enforced and pressed home upon their consciences. This is the best antidote to the poison.[31]

I find the *way of holiness* very narrow to walk in or to preach; and although I do not consider *sanctification—Christian perfection,* commonplace subjects, yet I make them the burden, and labour to make them the savour of every sermon.[32]

I am divinely impressed with a charge to preach sanctification in every sermon.[33]

We were careful to pray with the families where we stopped, exhorting all professors to holiness.[34]

Part of this later fixation on Christian perfection was due to his own age and ill health. By 1814 he was worn out and approaching death, all the more anxiously examining his own soul for the marks of full sanctification. But the greater part of the fixation

[29] April 14, 1779; JLFA, I, 299.
[30] February 7, 1782; JLFA, I, 420.
[31] February 21, 1782; JLFA, I, 421.
[32] March 7, 1803; JLFA, II, 383.
[33] January 7, 1814; JLFA, II, 751.
[34] March 2, 1814; JLFA, II, 753

was due to his awareness of the need to keep the Methodists religiously alive. They tended to move from joyous noise to lethargy. Asbury found Wesley's doctrine of Christian perfection a stimulant. Let him who has been justified now press on to be sanctified. That word was still going out to the elders in Asbury's broken wording in his last year of life.

> You, Brethren, feel your weakness, feel your danger, feel your duty, to keep all the traveling, all the local line in gospel order. Quarterly Meetings, Camp Meetings, Common Meetings, Prayer Meetings, in order. Enquire at Quarterly Meetings, of the leaders, for their class papers, and of the class meetings. Meet every society and class in your power, preach in every society once a year. Meet every society in every Circuit if possible. Preach alarmingly, report the great doctrines of the gospel, give sinners, seekers, backsliders, and believers. Be distinct in doctrines, as grades in grace, conviction, repentance, justification, regeneration and sanctification, distinct from justification. Oh what men of God we ought to be, and grace can make us so.[35]

Like most transplants from England, the doctrine grew a bit differently in American soil. The question was put to Wesley in 1744, "In what manner should we preach sanctification?" His cautious answer was, "Scarce at all to those who are not pressing forward: to those who are, always by way of promise; always *drawing* rather than *driving*." [36] Wesley came on a bit more strongly in 1764: "Therefore, all our preachers should make a point of preaching perfection to believers constantly, strongly, and explicitly; and all believers should mind this one thing, and continually agonise for it." [37] In 1774 he wrote to Thomas Rankin in America:

> I have been lately thinking a good deal on one point, wherein perhaps we have all been wanting. We have not made it a rule, as

---

[35] Quoted from *The Western Methodist*, April 25, 1834; reprinted in *Methodist History*, October, 1962, p. 57.
[36] *Plain Account of Christian Perfection*, p. 34.
[37] *Ibid.*, p. 100.

soon as ever persons were justified, to remind them of going on
to perfection. Whereas this is the very time preferable to all others.
. . . They have then the simplicity of little children, and they are
fervent in spirit, ready to cut off the right hand or to pluck out
the right eye. But if we once suffer this fervour to subside, we shall
find it hard enough to bring them again to this point.[38]

Here and in his letter of February 8, 1775, to Ann Bolton he
seems to say that new converts still in the flush of their conversion
experience ought to be led to expect a further experience in which
this "first love" would be "changed into pure love." [39] John Peters
sees this stress as going beyond Wesley's usual treatment of the doctrine.[40]

Such a stress was regular enough in America. On the American
frontier the doctrine was clearly to be used to put the heat on
those members who were "resting on their lees" or in any danger
of doing so. Asbury shows little restraint in pressing believers on
to an immediate experience of sanctification; his restraint appears
at the point of certifying those who claimed to have attained
it. Generally he makes a terse report of the number of those justified and those sanctified. Or he refers to "speakers" at a love feast
in such a way that one infers they were speaking some hope of having attained perfect love.

Our love feast lasted about two hours; some spoke of the sanctifying
grace of God.[41]

At the meeting we found some faithful souls, and the work revives
among them: they were greatly led out to speak in the love feast,
six or seven standing up as witnesses of a present salvation from
all sin.[42]

Sometimes his evaluations of the holiness claims verge on the
skeptical.

[38] LJW, VI, 103.
[39] LJW, VI, 138.
[40] *Christian Perfection and American Methodism*, p. 82.
[41] November 5, 1780; JLFA, I, 387.
[42] February 5, 1781; JLFA, I, 399.

> John Beauchamp and Dr. Bowness, both professed sanctification: I hope it is so. The society is much increased: but all is not gold that shines.[43]

> This family professeth sanctification; whether this be so in the fullest sense I know not; but this I know, that they are much more spiritual than ever I knew them: so far it is well, and we go upon safe ground.[44]

Certainly he was prepared to make plain the hazards of backsliding from such a pinnacle; Wesley had given superb material for this in his "Cautions and Directions given to the Greatest Professors in the Methodist Societies." [45]

The great value of the doctrine as Asbury and his preachers saw it was that the sinner was always under leverage; the screws were always on. There was no hiding place. The people must be kept keyed up until they were all the way to holiness. In fact, the people were obligated to key themselves up until they had completed this pilgrimage, and even then they dared not let up lest they lapse or backslide. Christ had already enabled all men for salvation, and now, for fear of eternal damnation, they must press on. The circuit rider and the camp meeting preacher always had his message. He must move the people to act on God's gracious gift. Revival, new creaturehood, justification were to be wrought. God's grace had gone ahead. Now the traveling preacher must fire the people to their work.

Wesley was also very cautious in answering his own question whether sanctification was instantaneous or not.

> In examining this, let us go on step by step.
> An instantaneous change has been wrought in some believers; none can deny this. Since that change they enjoy perfect love; they feel this, and this alone; they "rejoice evermore, pray without ceasing, and in everything give thanks." Now, this is all that I mean by perfection; therefore, these are witnesses of the perfection which I preach.

[43] February 22, 1780; JLFA, I, 337.
[44] April 28, 1780; JLFA, I, 347.
[45] *Plain Account of Christian Perfection*, pp. 86, 87-97.

"But in some this change was not instantaneous." They did not perceive the instant when it was wrought. It is often difficult to perceive the instant when a man dies; yet there is an instant in which life ceases. And if ever sin ceases, there must be a last moment of its existence, and a first moment of our deliverance from it.

"But if they have this love now, they will lose it." They may; but they need not. And whether they do or no, they have it now; they now experience what we teach. They now are all love; they now rejoice, pray, and praise without ceasing.

"However, sin is only suspended in them; it is not destroyed." Call it which you please. They are all love to-day; and they take no thought for the morrow.[46]

His point seems to be that this Christian perfection may come to the believer whether he knows it or not. It is instantaneous in the same sense that death is; it may come abruptly with smashing suddenness, or it may be almost impossible to isolate in time, although logically at some one moment the man is alive and at the next he is dead. Now this explanation does not give the force of "ought" to a smashing and joyously experienced moment of sanctification.

It is only natural that in the emotionally charged religious setting of America the focus should come to be on an identifiable experience of instantaneous sanctification. The member who was converted in a surge of feeling at a revival was likely to think of being sanctified in a surge of feeling at a revival. This line of thought found ready support from the revival preachers. For example, John Hagerty underwent a harrowing experience leading up to his conversion under the preaching of Methodists Isaac Rollins and John King. He expected his purification and Christian growth thereafter to be a "progressive work," until Methodist preacher Edward Dromgoole convinced him that his sanctification was to be another act of "simple faith" and that he was to "press hard after it." Then he underwent an equally harrowing experience leading up to his sanctification. After it all, he remained somewhat chastened but hopeful.

[46] *Ibid.*, pp. 106-7.

I do not know if I have felt anything contrary to love since. For some months my soul was continually happy. Not a cloud did arise to darken the skies. But afterwards through my rest being much broken by a Motherless infant I found much coldness and backwardness; but Glory be to my God He has delivered me from it, so that I enjoy a constant peace, and have a conscience void of offence towards God and man.[47]

Asbury was never fully satisfied that the preaching of sanctification was deeply enough established in his own time. He seemed to count it essential to the theological rationale of the continued revival and camp meeting he equated with Methodism. There is no hint that he ever suspected the eclipse of the doctrine and of the camp meeting together.

[47] Sweet, *Religion on the American Frontier*, IV, 125-28.

13
EPISCOPACY

As the man on the firing line in America, Asbury had to be ready to interpret and defend the place of a bishop in the Methodist Episcopal Church. From Anglican enemies of Methodism only the worst could be expected, and their opposition guaranteed an interminable literature of apology and rebuttal, of attack and reply. Even an Anglican friend like Devereux Jarratt found the new church order hard to bear. Methodists themselves entered into the opposition to episcopacy. William Guirey wrote a bitter attack;[1] O'Kelly was the raucous spokesman for some critics and the progenitor of many more. Charles Wesley contributed his acid lines on Asbury's ordination:

> A Roman emperor 'tis said,
> His favorite horse a consul made;
> But Coke brings greater things to pass,
> He makes a bishop of an ass.[2]

Asbury could do some leaning on John Wesley. That Methodist father seems to have been clear about the matter in his own mind.

---

[1] See JLFA, III, 22.
[2] JLFA, III, 65.

He was convinced by his studies of the writings of Peter King and Edward Stillingfleet. As he said in his letter to the Americans in 1784, "Lord King's *Account of the Primitive Church* convinced me many years ago that bishops and presbyters are the same order, and consequently have the same right to ordain." So he saw it entirely fitting that Anglican presbyter Wesley, assisted by presbyters Coke and Creighton, should ordain Whatcoat and Vasey to be presbyters.[3]

He seems to have been equally clear about the office of superintendent. The public certificate said:

> And therefore under the Protection of Almighty God, and with a single eye to his glory, I have this day set apart as a Superintendent, by the imposition of my hands and prayer (being assisted by other ordained ministers) Thomas Coke, Doctor of Civil Law, a Presbyter of the Church of England and man whom I judge to be well qualified for that great work.[4]

However, in his *Journal* for that day Wesley used the word "ordain" to describe what he had done, and the word "ordain" appeared in the service book he sent over to guide the setting apart of future elders and superintendents. Both Charles Wesley and Thomas Coke seem to have understood that Wesley meant to ordain a bishop.[5]

Wesley understood that ordination as a superintendent or bishop did not confer any sacerdotal powers; the presbyter could already administer sacraments. Ordination as a superintendent did not confer any ordaining power; the presbyter and bishop were of the same order and had power to ordain. Ordination as a superintendent was an administrative matter, the naming of a man to maintain Wesleyan order in the church. Wesley almost certainly expected that during his lifetime he would choose the American superintendents and they would be under his direction. He delib-

[3] See HAM, I, 197-202; Norman W. Spellmann, "The General Superintendency in American Methodism 1784-1870" (Unpublished dissertation, Yale University, 1961), pp. 52-63.

[4] Wesley, *Journal*, VII, facsimile facing p. 16.

[5] See HAM, I, 204-6.

erately avoided the use of the title "bishop" and was incensed when the Americans did not follow his lead.

Asbury, however, had to have his own rationale and his personal apologetic. The critics leveled their attacks directly at him and he must answer. Further, he did not agree with Wesley altogether in this matter of episcopacy, and he had redirected Wesley's plan from its very beginnings in America. He agreed with Wesley that presbyters possess the right of ordination; there was no doubt of the validity of what Wesley and his assistants had done. But he differed at two crucial points. First, the superintendents in America would have to be directly chosen by the American preachers. Therefore their ultimate direction would come from the General Conference and not from Wesley or from England. In this Asbury recognized the American mind-set for independence. Election was essential, even if it was to be for life. Second, bishops and presbyters were not really of the same order, as Wesley claimed. Rather, there were three orders of the ministry: bishops, elders, and deacons.

> The God of glory cover your assembly and direct all your acts and deliberations for the Apostolic order and establishment of the Church of God in holy succession to the end of time. Only recollect as far as your observation or information will go, what God has done by us in Europe and America in about 70 years in Europe, and less than 50 years in America, and what wonderful things he may do for us and our successors in future years if we stand fast in the Gospel doctrine and pure Apostolic ordination, discipline and government into which we have been called and now stand.
>
> We are prepared, and, if called upon, to prove and demonstrate even in your assembly, not from uncertain Church Histories and testimonies, but from the pure Oracles of the New Testament,— Three distinct ordinations, their distinct powers rising in gospel order by constituted degrees, one over another, and under the government, and distinct in names, that is to say Apostles, Elders, and Deacons. We will enter the sanctuary of divine truth, here we stand, this is our ground.[6]

[6] Address to the General Conference of 1816; JLFA, III, 532.

Nor would it do to say that all elders (used synonymously with presbyters) were equal except that the bishop presides and administers. In what sense can a permanent president be said to be equal with others?

> I recollect having read, some years since, Ostervald's Christian Theology: having a wish to transcribe a few sentiments in the work, I met with it, and extracted from chap. 2, page 317, what follows. "Yet it cannot be denied that in the primitive Church there was always a president who presided over others, who were in a state of equality with himself: this is clearly proved from the catalogues of bishops to be found in Eusebius and others; in them we may see the names of the bishops belonging to the principal Churches, many of whom were ordained whilst the apostles (but especially John) were still living." So far Mr. Ostervald, who, I presume, was a Presbyterian. In Cave's Lives of the Fathers, and in the writings of the ancients, it will appear that the Churches of Alexandria, and elsewhere, had large congregations, many elders; that the apostles might appoint and ordain bishops. Mr. Ostervald, who, it appears, is a candid and well-informed man, has gone as far as might be expected for a Presbyterian. For myself, I see but a hair's breadth difference between the sentiments of the respectable and learned author of Christian Theology, and the practice of the Methodist Episcopal Church. There is not—nor indeed, in my mind, can there be—a perfect equality between a constant president, and those over whom he always presides.[7]

Perhaps he never fully resolved his own confusion on the question whether every bishop holds superiority in order or whether he is simply first among equals. He could hardly illustrate by his own case; everyone came to count him unique—as one with apostolic commission to found a church along with Wesley. But his own operation indicates that he felt ordination as bishop conferred both ecclesiastical order and individual authority.[8]

He had recovered rather quickly from his "shock" at the

[7] April 5, 1801; JLFA, II, 289-90.
[8] See Spellmann, "General Superintendency," pp. 136-37, 150-59; Barton, "Definition of the Episcopal Office in American Methodism," pp. 34-58.

thought of being a bishop in the Methodist Episcopal Church. He learned rather quickly to hand back some answers to his critics. He had not, he claimed, ever insisted on being addressed as "bishop," as O'Kelly charged; rather, the preachers in the conference sessions had weighed the perennial question of the use of such clergy titles as "Mr." or "Reverend," and decided it was best to give every man his precise official title of deacon or elder or bishop.[9] So Asbury was "Bishop Asbury" in name as he saw it. For those who questioned his authority, he had an answer:

> I will tell the world what I rest my authority upon. 1. Divine authority. 2. Seniority in America. 3. The election of the General Conference. 4. My ordination by Thomas Coke, William Philip Otterbein, German Presbyterian minister, Richard Whatcoat, and Thomas Vasey. 5. Because the signs of an apostle have been seen in me.[10]

So it was in the very midst of his service as bishop that he was working out his own understanding of the office. He stood with those American preachers who detached themselves from English direction. He stood against those American preachers who would weaken the episcopal power; instead of allowing election of presiding elders he developed an eldership which was really a part of the bishop's administrative system. After the General Conference of 1808 he could breathe a little easier. At least his whole episcopal structure could not now be thrown out by a bare majority in one conference because the Third Restrictive Rule passed by that conference said: "They shall not change or alter any part or rule of our government, so as to do away episcopacy, or to destroy the plan of our itinerant general superintendency." [11]

All the while he was thinking and reading and formulating. He and Coke justified episcopacy in the examples of traveling bishops Timothy and Titus in the New Testament. They saw themselves as "chief executor of those regulations, which were

---

[9] Leroy Lee, *Life of Jesse Lee*, p. 279.

[10] May 22, 1805; JLFA, II, 469-70.

[11] *Journals of the General Conference . . . 1796-1836*, pp. 82-83.

made in the college of presbyters." They pointed out that their authority was much less than that of Wesley in England, notably in their being subject to the direction of General Conference.[12]

"The feeling of uncertainty about the authenticity of the Methodist episcopacy gave rise to a long series of writings on the subject. Ezekiel Cooper at one time prepared a treatise and engaged in rather exhaustive research on the whole history of episcopacy. He prepared a series of essays in the form of epistles to Asbury on the subject, probably with an eye to eventual publication." [13]

Then Asbury recapitulated it all, with some fascinating additions, in his long "Valedictory Address to William McKendree" in a letter dated August 5, 1813.[14] This is his summary of the matter, his contribution to the ongoing church. It is evidently meant for publication.

> Speaking to the Genesee Annual Conference in your presence on the subject of apostolical, missionary, Methodist Episcopal Church government, I was desired to commit my thoughts to writing. I feel the more disposed to do this that I may leave a written testimony which may be seen read and known when your friend and father is taken from the evil to come.

On his deathbed he was asked if he had anything to communicate. He said he had expressed his mind on the order of the church in this address to McKendree. "I wish to warn you against the growing evil of locality in bishops, elders, preachers, or Conferences." Cities will always tend to settle a minister. They have the money to "purchase" a minister and there are always able men who will put themselves up for sale. Asbury sided clearly against the cities which create such havoc and in favor of the circuit pattern of the country. This aversion to "locality" is of one piece with his theory of church order.

Now follows his understanding of the history of church order. The whole thesis is in one paragraph.

[12] *Discipline*, 1798, pp. 40-46.

[13] Frederick A. Norwood, "The Church Takes Shape," HAM, I, 460.

[14] JLFA, III, 475-92. Asbury's comments in the following pages are all taken from this important document.

I am bold to say that the apostolic order of things was lost in the first century, when Church governments were adulterated and had much corruption attached to them. At the Reformation the reformers only beat off a part of the rubbish which put a stop to the rapid increase of absurdities at that time; but how they have increased since! Recollect the state of the different Churches, as it respects government and discipline in the seventeenth century when the Lord raised up that great and good man, John Wesley, who formed an evangelical society in England. In 1784, an apostolical form of Church government was formed in the United States of America at the first General Conference of the Methodist Episcopal Church held at Baltimore, in the State of Maryland.

So the apostolic order was lost in the first century. Wesley and his assisting presbyters restored it at Bristol in 1784. And the new lineage of proper bishops was Wesley, Coke, Asbury, Whatcoat, and McKendree.

The address continues with several replies which must be made to opponents. Some say we cannot have such doctrines, convictions, conversions, witnesses of sanctification, and holy men as there were in apostolic times. Asbury replies that we can, we must, and the Methodists do have precisely these apostolic marks. Some others want to justify a settled ministry. But what can be said for these learned, parent-dominated, proud, money-loving clergy who do not *go* to preach, as an apostle is *sent*, but *stay* to preach. They are a different breed from the Methodists and from the ministers in the Acts of the Apostles, including Paul, Timothy, and Titus. So how could the Methodists ask or take their church order either from the present episcopal churches (Latin, Greek, English, Lutheran, Swedish, Protestant Episcopal) or from the nonepiscopal groups (Presbyterians, Independents, Baptists, Quakers)? They are all hopelessly infected with "locality."

It will be seen that we are so unlike them that we could not stand as related to them. Would their bishops ride five or six thousand miles in nine months for eighty dollars a year, with their traveling expense less or more, preach daily when opportunity serves, meet a number of camp meetings in the year, make arrangements for stationing seven hundred preachers, ordain a hundred more annually, ride through all kinds of weather, and along roads in the worst state, at our time of life—the one sixty-nine, the other in his fifty-sixth year?

Or could we subscribe to Calvinian articles? Surely, no. Or could we submit to locality? By no means. Let local men ordain local men, baptize, or rebaptize local men; we must shape our course otherwise and prepare to meet the different Annual Conferences from Maine to Georgia and the Mississippi, and to retain all the ancient essential branches of Methodism in all its parts and try sacredly to maintain our traveling plan and support a true missionary, apostolic Church.

As for those Methodists who do not show proper respect for the restored apostolic order, let them remember:

It is a serious thing for a bishop to be stripped of any constitutional rights chartered to him at his ordination, without which he could not and would not have entered into that sacred office, he being conscious at the same time he had never violated those sacred rights. Comparing human Church history with the Acts of the Apostles, it will manifestly appear that the apostolic order of things ended in about fifty years. With the preachers and people of that day, the golden order was lost. But we must restore and retain primitive order; we must, we will, have the same doctrine, the same spirituality, the same power in ordinances, in ordination, and in spirit.

There may be an occasional apostate among so many Methodists, but this does not invalidate the obviously apostolic plan. If the primitive church declined from purity, that is no sign that the restored order must decline. "We live in a purer age and in a free country. . . . We have lived to see the end of such persons who left us and set up for themselves—witness Hammett and O'Kelly."

In the course of a long annotated citation from Thomas Haweis in support of his position Asbury clearly indicates what is for him the basic mark of a true bishop. He is a worthy Christian called of God to *itinerate*. And *itinerancy* is absolutely crucial. Formal learning cannot be assumed among apostles; there are many illustrations of the prideful abuse of learning. But the true apostolate is the traveling apostolate; consider, for example, Peter, Paul, Timothy, and Titus.

This leads me to conclude that there were no local bishops until the second century; that the apostles, in service, were bishops, and that those who were ordained in the second century mistook their calling when they became local and should have followed those bright examples in the apostolic age.

It is my confirmed opinion that the apostles acted both as bishops and traveling superintendents in planting and watering, ruling and ordering the whole connection; and that they did not ordain any local bishops, but that they ordained local deacons and elders. I feel satisfied we should do the same.

By this criterion it is the Methodists who carry on the true apostolic order.

My dear Bishop, it is the traveling apostolic order and ministry that is found in our very constitution. No man among us can locate without order, or forfeit his official standing. No preacher is stationary more than two years; no presiding elder more than four years; and the constitution will remove them; and all are movable at the pleasure of the superintendent whenever he may find it necessary for the good of the cause.

By mileage traveled in conscientious oversight, Asbury and his colleagues were without challenge the true bishops.

Let Presbyterians say and write what they may, as if episcopacy never existed, it must be granted that in the first, second, and third centuries many of the bishops were holy men, who traveled and labored in the ministry very extensively, not unlike their grand pattern, St. Paul, and the other holy apostolical men, of which we have good historical evidence, which is all the evidence that can now be given. To the people of our day we give ocular demonstration, and the generations to come may read our Church records and Conference journals, where they shall see what vast tracts of country we traveled over in visiting the nine Conferences annually.

It is plain that Asbury did not lay his episcopal claim through any uninterrupted chain of apostolic succession. Wesley had broken with that as a fiction as early as 1746; Asbury found Wesley completely convincing on the subject.[15] Nor was the garb of a bishop essential. He could lay that aside in deference to the frontier bias of his constituency without any serious sense of loss. Keeping the continuity of worship, rite, and sacrament as a heritage of the church was not the essential episcopal function for Asbury; he seems to have celebrated the sacraments gladly and to have ordained preachers as was his duty, but he could dispense with regular use of Wesley's *Sunday Service* in favor of the roaring extemporaneousness of aroused Americans. There was the body of Methodist doctrine which was Anglican and Wesleyan; Asbury guarded and promoted it, but he hardly made the personification of orthodox doctrine his episcopal role. It was itinerancy and administration which necessarily marked a bishop, and both were essential marks as he saw them.

> With us a bishop is a plain man, altogether like his brethren, wearing no marks of distinction, advanced in age, and by virtue of his office can sit as president in all the solemn assemblies of the ministers of the gospel; and many times, if he is able, called upon to labor and suffer more than any of his brethren; no negative or positive in forming Church rules; raised to a small degree of constituted and elective authority above all his brethren; and in the executive department, power to say, "Brother, that must not be, that cannot be," having full power to put a negative or a positive in his high charge of administration.[16]

The year Asbury died, he was describing to the conference the kind of man to be sought as a Methodist bishop.

> Your governors shall come forth out of yourselves, and the Holy Ghost shall direct your choice as in the Antiochian Conference. . . . They must be formed in all things after the pattern shewed us in the mount, able Ministers of the New Testament, real Apostolic

[15] *Discipline*, 1798, p. 46.
[16] To Joseph Benson, January 15, 1816; JLFA, III, 544-45.

men filled with the Holy Ghost. But what does our order of things require of them? Not such as can be performed by superannuated or supernumerary preachers, but by men just past the meridian, that have already proved themselves not only servants but mere slaves, *who* with willing minds have taken with cheerfulness and resignation frontier stations, with hard fare, labouring and suffering night and day, hazarding their lives by waters, by lodging indoors and out, and where Indian depredations and murders have been committed once a month or perhaps once a quarter. . . . They ought to be men who can ride at least three thousand miles and meet ten or eleven Conferences in a year, and by their having had a charge of local Conferences from sixty to an hundred Official characters, to have presided in and *to have* directed well all the business of the whole with every member, having received and graduated exhorters, preachers, deacons, and elders in the local line, ready to all the duties of their calling, always pleasant, affable, and communicative,—to know how to behave in all company, rich or poor, impious or pious, ministers and professors of our own and all denominations, but more abundantly to remember to the poor the gospel must be preached, and always to condescend to men of low estate.[17]

This was his ideal of an apostolic bishop. It was, though not intentionally, his portrait of himself twenty years younger.

One further test of apostolicity was at work in the minds of many of the preachers and the people. This was the test of success. The personal effectiveness of Asbury and the fruitfulness of the itinerant system defended episcopacy. No church grew like the Methodist Episcopal Church. Asbury, who insisted on being a sort of martyr himself and often enough presented the Methodists as a pure but persecuted remnant, also advanced as proof of divine approbation and proper order the "manifest approval by the people." The emphases stand side by side in his letters: "If we have no other mark of Apostles, we shall have *poverty, reproach* and *hard labor,*" but "rich men are coming in, and bringing their *daughters.*" [18]

---

[17] Address to the General Conference; JLFA, III, 540-41.
[18] To Thomas L. Douglass, January 25, 1810; *Methodist History*, October, 1962, p. 46.

14
SLAVERY

When Asbury as a young man left England, the Methodist position on slavery was already clear. Slavery did not exist in England and the English Methodists did not want it to exist anywhere. The evangelical Wesley wrote to the evangelical Wilberforce in Parliament: "O, be not weary of well doing! Go on, in the name of God and in the power of His might, till even American slavery (the vilest that ever saw the sun) shall vanish away before it." [1] Wesley's *Thoughts upon Slavery*, published in 1774, gave shape and support to the antislavery sentiment which was general in Methodist societies. Slave procurement was awful inhumanity; slave trading was degrading and cruel. "I absolutely deny all slave-holding to be consistent with any degree of natural justice." It was also "utterly inconsistent with mercy" and incompatible with any claim to godliness. [2]

However, when Asbury came to America he found his most fertile field for evangelism in the southern colonies. He loved

[1] To William Wilberforce, February 24, 1791; LJW, VIII, 265.
[2] *The Works of John Wesley*, ed. Thomas Jackson (Grand Rapids: Zondervan, 1958), XI, 59-79.

the piety of these southern converts and their openness to Methodist revival. But many of them were slaveholders who intended to remain slaveholders. They saw no necessary conflict between vital religion and slavery. "Methodists, Baptists, Presbyterians, in the highest flights of rapturous piety, still maintain and defend it." [3] Eventually Asbury had to take them with slavery or not have them at all.

He did not give up easily. With the support of some zealous American preachers like Freeborn Garrettson, who had emancipated his own slaves, he attempted to act against the evil. In 1780 Asbury was presiding over a conference of seventeen ministers at Baltimore. The first official action of American Methodists against slavery was taken.

Quest. 16. Ought not this Conference to require those travelling preachers who hold slaves to give promises to set them free?
Yes

Quest. 17. Does this Conference acknowledge that slavery is contrary to the law of God, man, and nature, and hurtful to society; contrary to the dictates of conscience and pure religion, and doing that which we would not others should do to us and ours? Do we pass our disapprobation on all our friends who keep slaves, and advise their freedom?
Yes[4]

The language here was mandatory for itinerants but only a strong admonition for the local preachers and laity. It is likely that a few slaves were freed because of this stirring of the issue; traveling preacher Philip Gatch emancipated his. Grumbling non-compliance was more general.

At the conference of 1783 they tried again:

Quest. 10. What shall be done with our local preachers who hold slaves contrary to the laws which authorize their freedom in any of the United States?

[3] January 9, 1798; JLFA, II, 151.
[4] *Minutes of the Annual Conferences . . . 1773-1828*, p. 12.

We will try them another year. In the mean time let every assistant deal faithfully and plainly with every one, and report to the next Conference. It may then be necessary to suspend them.[5]

Asbury said of the 1783 conference at Ellis' Chapel, "We all agreed in the spirit of African liberty, and strong testimonies were borne in its favour in our love feast."[6] However, the exceptions seem more notable than the compliance. When the question was put in 1784 about local preachers who would not emancipate slaves, the action was "try those in Virginia another year, and suspend the preachers in Maryland, Delaware, Pennsylvania, and New-Jersey."[7] So the deep southerners were exempt because their state laws did not allow manumission, Virginians were to be handled gently, and the pressure was applied in the north, where the problem was minimal among the preachers anyway.

Thomas Coke was a key man in the Christmas Conference of 1784 and he was a zealous foe of slavery. Thus reinforced, Asbury and the American preachers took drastic antislavery action for the newly formed Methodist Episcopal Church. They declared the institution "contrary to the golden law of God . . . and the inalienable Rights of Mankind, as well as every Principle of the Revolution." Then they pressed for immediate and effective action "to extirpate this Abomination from among us" and drew up an actual scheme for emancipation. Methodists who refused to comply were given twelve months to withdraw from the societies, after being notified to free their slaves, or they were to be put out. No slaveholders were to be admitted to membership until they had signed a deed of emancipation. For members in states with laws against emancipation, grudging exception was made. Special consideration was also given to Virginia's strong slavery tradition, although its laws technically allowed manumission. The ban on the buying and selling of slaves was continued, unless they were bought for the

[5] *Ibid.*, p. 18.
[6] May 7, 1783; JLFA, I, 441.
[7] *Minutes of the Annual Conferences . . . 1773-1828*, p. 20.

purpose of setting them free. No Methodist was to give away his slaves for the purpose of keeping them in bondage.[8]

They could not make this position stick. Asbury and Coke bravely tried to do it. They circulated petitions to send to the Virginia State Assembly and to the Legislature of North Carolina asking immediate or gradual emancipaton of slaves.[9] Coke's *Journal* says that Asbury personally visited the governor of North Carolina on behalf of the petition and "gained him over," but no legislation appeared from it all.[10] They personally called on George Washington and solicited his aid in the abolition project. Washington offered them hospitality, deplored slavery, but courteously declined to press their petition.[11] Coke sounded off against slavery in Virginia pulpits; he was threatened with mob violence, and bills of indictment were presented against him in at least two counties.

Opposition soon arose within the church. Jesse Lee rebuked Coke for speaking harshly against slavery at the conference in April of 1785. After another conference about two weeks later Asbury recounts:

> I found the minds of the people greatly agitated with our rules against slavery, and a proposed petition to the general assembly for the emancipation of the blacks. Colonel Bedford and Doctor Coke disputed on the subject, and the Colonel used some threats: next day, brother O'Kelly let fly at them, and they were made angry enough; we, however, came off with whole bones.[12]

Coke began to yield to the pressures. Before expressing his sentiments against slavery he would be careful to address the Negroes on the duty of servants to their masters. Finally he went so far as to state that he should not have used the pulpit to attack

---

[8] *Discipline*, 1785, pp. 14-15.

[9] April 30 and November 15, 1785; JLFA, I, 488, 498; *Extracts of the Journals of the Late Rev. Thomas Coke* (Dublin: Methodist Book Room, 1816), p. 67.

[10] April 19, 1785; *Extracts of the Journals*, pp. 65-66.

[11] Coke, *Extracts of the Journals*, p. 73.

[12] April 30, 1785; JLFA, I, 488.

slavery.[13] Just as Coke was ready to sail back to England, the 1785 conference at Baltimore considered slavery again. The stout declaration of the Christmas Conference was but five months old. Coke records its fate:

> We thought it prudent to suspend the minute concerning slavery, on account of the great opposition that had been given it, our work being in too infantile a state to push things to extremity. However, we were agreeably informed that several of our friends in *Maryland* had already emancipated their slaves.[14]

What was left in the 1785 Minutes was a plain but toothless statement: "We do hold in the deepest abhorrence the practice of slavery; and shall not cease to seek its destruction by all wise and prudent means." [15]

Asbury did not cease to try. When the General Rules were printed in the *Discipline* for the first time in 1789, they were not submitted to any conference for approval and there was a new rule added which had not been needed by Wesley. It forbade "the buying or selling the bodies and souls of men, women or children, with an intention to enslave them." [16] Asbury commended the Presbyterian minister David Rice for his efforts to keep slavery out of Kentucky.[17] At Lane's Chapel in Virginia he was encouraged because "slavery is greatly on the decline among them." [18] But some citizens of Charleston, South Carolina, intended to give him neither cooperation nor peace.

> While another was speaking in the morning to a very crowded house, and many outside, a man made a riot at the door; an alarm at once took place; the ladies leaped out at the windows of the church, and a dreadful confusion ensued. Again whilst I was speaking at night, a stone was thrown against the north side of the

[13] Coke, *Extracts of the Journals*, p. 95.
[14] *Ibid.*, p. 74.
[15] *Minutes of the Annual Conferences . . . 1773-1828*, p. 24.
[16] *Discipline*, 1789, p. 48.
[17] April 10, 1792; JLFA, I, 712.
[18] January 11, 1789; JLFA, I, 590.

church; then another on the south; a third came through the pulpit
window, and struck near me inside the pulpit. I however continued
to speak on; my subject, "How beautiful upon the mountains," &c.[19]

We had an unkind attack published against us relative to our slave
rules; it was answered to purpose. I had not much doubt who the
author of this unworthy work was.[20]

Finally he too began to yield. If there had to be a decision between working at antislavery agitation and working at evangelization of the south, it was clear where his choice lay. Evangelization
must come first. He became increasingly convinced that a choice
must be made in these terms. The economic drive for slavery was
plain. Spinning and weaving machines could be fed by the new
cotton gins, but feeding the gins took field hands. The price of
slaves kept rising.

We have been working this week from Saluda to Reedy River, down
the Enoree, crossing and recrossing through Pendleton, Greensville,
Laurens, Spartanburg, and Newbury counties in South Carolina. I
cannot record great things upon religion in this quarter; *but cotton
sells high.* I fear there is more gold than grace—more of silver than
of "that wisdom that cometh from above." [21]

The General Conferences of 1796 and 1800 deplored the evils
of slavery but would take no direct action to eradicate it. The
traveling preachers must free their slaves; one suspects there were
not many traveling preachers who owned any. As for the laity,
there was only admonition. Each annual conference was allowed
to decide whether it would permit slaveholders to be officers in
its churches. Under these circumstances local option on slavery
would be the practice, and southerners would opt to keep it
with limitations. When the General Conference of 1804 acted to
refer the subject of slavery to the bishops so they might "form a

[19] March 14, 1788; JLFA, I, 564.
[20] March 17-19, 1789; JLFA, I, 594.
[21] October 24, 1801; JLFA, II, 311.

section to suit the southern and northern states, as they in their
wisdom may think best," Asbury declined to serve.[22] No statement was going to suit Methodists of both south and north, and
he knew it. At the 1808 General Conference Asbury moved from
the chair "that there be one thousand forms of Discipline prepared
for use of the South Carolina Conference, in which the section
and rule on slavery be left out." [23]

Silence on slavery in return for the right to work in the south
was to be his mature policy.

> I am brought to conclude that slavery will exist in Virginia perhaps
> for ages; there is not a sufficient sense of religion nor of liberty to
> destroy it.[24]

> We are defrauded of great numbers by the pains that are taken to
> keep the blacks from us; their masters are afraid of the influence of
> our principles. Would not an *amelioration* in the condition and
> treatment of slaves have produced more practical good to the poor
> Africans, than any attempt at their *emancipation?* The state of
> society, unhappily, does not admit of this: besides, the blacks are
> deprived of the means of instruction; who will take the pains to lead
> them into the way of salvation, and watch over them that they
> may not stray, but the Methodists? Well; now their masters will
> not let them come to hear us. What is the personal liberty of the
> African which he may abuse, to the salvation of his soul; how may
> it be compared? [25]

But it always rankled in his soul. While he received the hospitality
of large landholders, he was grumbling to his *Journal:*

> O! to be dependent on slaveholders is in part to be a slave, and
> I was free born.[26]

[22] *Journals of the General Conference . . . 1796-1836,* p. 60.
[23] *Ibid.,* p. 93.
[24] January 9, 1798; JLFA, II, 151.
[25] February 1, 1809; JLFA, II, 591.
[26] January 9, 1798; JLFA, II, 151.

The rich among the people never thought us worthy to preach to them: they did indeed give their slaves liberty to hear and join our Church; but now it appears the poor Africans will no longer have this indulgence. Perhaps we shall soon be thought unfit for the company of their dogs.[27]

My mind is grieved with the *old sore* in Virginia; but I must bear it patiently.[28]

I saw how the flood had ploughed up the street of Augusta: I walked over the ruins for nearly two miles, viewing the deep gulfs in the main street. I suppose they would crucify me if I were to tell them it is the African flood; but if they could hear me think, they would discover this to be my sentiment.[29]

Polygamy, slavery, and such like were never commanded under this dispensation, but only tolerated, and accompanied by strict injunctions to prevent men from running to greater lengths in these practices. . . . Polygamy was allowed to prevent general whoredom. Servitude was regulated to prevent slavery and oppression, death, and loss of limbs. If any had asked the Lord on the subject of slavery, as on polygamy, he must have said, Moses, as a man, suffered this, a less evil, to prevent a greater; but it was not so from the beginning of the creation: it is the fall which hath done this, not a holy God. It is man's work, of two evils to choose the least. But God is not tempted of us to evil, neither tempteth he any man. Christians, of two evils should not choose or use either, if they would be like God.[30]

Increasingly, then, he shifted from attempts to emancipate the Negroes to attempts to evangelize the Negroes. As it became plain that his interest was "spiritual," he was allowed to preach to both Negroes and whites.

Our tabernacle is crowded again: the minds of the people are strangely changed; and the indignation excited against us is over-

[27] January 30, 1801; JLFA, II, 281.
[28] December 14, 1797; JLFA, II, 142.
[29] March 10, 1796; JLFA, II, 80.
[30] January 1, 1798; JLFA, II, 149.

past: the people see and confess that the slaves are made better by religion; and wonder to hear the poor Africans pray and exhort.[31]

The *Journal* presents an amazing and increasingly biracial ministry. Scores of entries speak of the numbers in the congregations "whites and blacks."

I continued a week in Charleston, lodging in our own house at Bethel, receiving my visitors, ministers and people, white, black, and yellow.[32]

The Baptists have built an elegant church, planned for a steeple and organ: they take the rich; and the commonalty and the slaves fall to us: this is well. We have about twenty whites, and between three and four hundred blacks in society here.[33]

A late camp meeting upon Town Creek has given a revival to religion amongst both whites and blacks.[34]

It seems plain that sometimes the whites and blacks were together in the same church buildings, sometimes the Negroes on a farm were specially gathered by the owner to hear preaching, and sometimes there were voluntary all-Negro gatherings for religious services.[35] Asbury was aware of the small prestige of the Negro gatherings, but he seems to have worked with them happily. In 1810 there were 34,724 Negroes in full Methodist membership.

Racial tensions in the church were not limited to the south. At St. George's Church in Philadelphia, Lovely Lane Church in Baltimore, and John Street Church in New York the Negro members became dissatisfied with their treatment. They were expected to take side seats or were forcibly relegated to the balcony. They were allowed Communion only after all whites had been served. Their preachers were seldom allowed to preach to the whites. Out-

[31] February 25, 1801; JLFA, II, 284.
[32] November 20, 1803; JLFA, II, 414.
[33] January 27, 1804; JLFA, II, 423-24.
[34] February 11, 1804; JLFA, II, 425.
[35] See December 3, 1809, and February 3 and 5, 1796; JLFA, II, 621-22, 77.

standing among the Negro preachers were Richard Allen of Philadelphia and Daniel Coker of Baltimore, both ordained as deacons
by Asbury. When the Negroes began to meet separately from the
whites they counted Asbury as a friend. He saw to it that their
societies were supplied with preaching and sacraments; he helped
by dedicating their new meeting places and by preaching in them.
One separating Negro group in New York built a sanctuary on
Elizabeth Street and called it Asbury Church. During Asbury's
ministry these Negro Methodist churches were in full connection
with and under administrative control of the Methodist Episcopal
Church. Only in the year of his death was the African Methodist
Episcopal Church organized as a separate denomination at Philadelphia; the African Methodist Episcopal Zion Church held its
first conference in New York five years later. One can only speculate about Asbury's loyalties here. How would he have chosen between his desire for the free advancement of Negroes and his
desire for one Methodist episcopate for America? Perhaps his early
encouragement to the Negro Methodist churches was one of the
most socially significant works of his life.

15
METHODIST SUPERIORITY

Francis Asbury found it very difficult to be patient with non-Methodists. It was bad enough that some marginal Methodists should backslide; that some people should remain non-Methodists by choice was ultimately intolerable. He did not hunger for controversy; there was little of the belligerent cockiness of Peter Cartwright in him. He simply viewed it as natural that everybody should be a Methodist without argument. If some must argue, they were to be borne with until God's logic overcame them.

After all, the aim of the Methodists was to renew the "work of God." Asbury was the marked prophet of the new work: "Surely God sent me to these people at the first." [1] The goal was that all souls be converted and prepared for heaven. In the meantime things could be mightily improved here on earth by eliminating slavery and whiskey and by increasing holiness everywhere. The business of invading the parish bounds of other ministers had been pretty well rationalized by the Methodists in England.[2] Outside

[1] February 21, 1772; JLFA, I, 20.
[2] See HAM, I, 21.

of New England there was no appreciable parish structure in America. Asbury and his troops simply moved in everywhere. If they were welcomed, they made Methodists of everybody in sight; if they were opposed, they did the same; if they were ignored, they did the same.

Most American people were unchurched. Certainly, according to Asbury's standards, they had no basis for resisting the Methodists. "Some, it appeared, had not heard a sermon for half a year; such a famine there is of the word in these parts, and a still greater one of the *pure* word." [3] Unless they repented and were saved, they were lost. If they resisted, they were resisting God. To these holdouts the preachers must go and go again, no matter what the hardships or persecutions.

> I reflect upon the present ruin of the Orphan House [Whitefield's]; and taking a view of the money expended, the persons employed, the preachers sent over, I was led to inquire, where are they? and how has it sped? The earth, the army, the Baptists, the Church, the Independents, have swallowed them all up at this *windmill end of the continent.* A wretched country this!—but there are souls, precious souls, worth worlds. [4]

Asbury saw some good among the Anglicans. He himself had been a faithful Anglican and had urged his early constituents to attend Anglican services. [5] There were evangelicals among Anglican clergymen who befriended the Methodists—Stringer, Magaw, Jarratt, Pettigrew, Ogden. Many Methodist members came from the ranks of the nominal Anglicans. At one stage Asbury may have had an idea that Anglicans and Methodists in America might unite; the Methodists had the gospel and the people while the Anglicans had the orders. But the Anglicans as an establishment or a denomination would never displace the Methodists, as Asbury saw it. Said he, "Attended the old church, as usual, but clearly

[3] February 21, 1772; JLFA, I, 20.
[4] February 2, 1793; JLFA, I, 746.
[5] May 22, 1780; JLFA, I, 352.

saw where the Gospel ministry was." [6] Anglican clergy were long
on formal learning and short on feeling; such a gospel would
never move America. Even when an Anglican preached a good
sermon, which was rare enough, he failed to follow it up with
exhortation and proper discipline of converts. Anglicans had only
a handful of preachers, while their bishops and even rectors acted
more like prelates than like the poor itinerants they ought to be.
Sometimes, in the early days, they actually tried to prevent
Methodist preaching.[7] The great work of God could not be
entrusted to these hands.

There was also some good among the Quakers. There was no
denying the simplicity and piety of many of them. They were
usually kind hosts and made good Methodist converts. And concerning slavery they were exemplary.

> I find the more pious part of the people called Quakers, are exerting
> themselves for the liberation of the slaves. This is a very laudable
> design; and what the Methodists must come to, or, I fear, the Lord
> will depart from them.[8]

But many of them had lost discipline and gone worldly. Asbury
viewed them as "fallen from their former lively and spiritual
state." [9] He wrote, "The Presbyterians have reformed; the Episcopalians and the Methodists; why should not the Friends?" and
then added a sizable page of suggested reforms designed to make
them operate like Methodists.[10] They were prone to argue with
the Methodists. "Brother Watters went to a Quaker meeting, and
began to speak; but some of the Friends desired him to sit down." [11]
When one Quaker thought the Methodists should dispense with
sacraments entirely, since they were not essential to salvation,
Asbury commented sourly to his *Journal* about unessential Quaker

[6] June 5, 1774; JLFA, I, 117-18.
[7] See December 11, 1772; JLFA, I, 57-58.
[8] June 10, 1778; JLFA, I, 273-74.
[9] November 21, 1772; JLFA, I, 54.
[10] To a Quaker, July, 1790; JLFA, III, 86-87.
[11] May 18, 1776; JLFA, I, 187.

usages like special garb and special language: "But what makes
them so contracted and bitter in their spirit as some of them
are?" [12] Nor did he see how some of them could deny that the
Scriptures are the grand criterion of all inward and outward religion. To deny this would oppose the present dictates of the Spirit
with his former dictates, "a most dangerous absurdity." [13] Quaker
meetings did not impress him; he "wondered to see so many sensible
men sit to hear two or three old women talk." [14] Asbury usually
felt some irritation whenever he brushed closely with Quaker practice: "We stopped to feed our horses at a Quaker preacher's, a
friend Nixon: we would not eat ourselves, where it was not agree-
able we should pray." [15] The great work of God for America could
not be expected from these.

It was easy for Asbury to recognize the kinship of Methodists
with Moravians:

> My heart was much taken up with God. I drank tea this afternoon
> with an old Moravian, who belonged to their fraternity in Fetter
> Lane, at the time when Mr. Wesley was so intimate with them.[16]

But generally the relationship was pretty thin. Asbury thought
they had gone to seed: "I heard a Moravian preach; but it was
only a historical faith." At their town of Salem, North Carolina, he
admired their industry: "Every one appeared to be in business." [17]
When he visited Moravian settlements in Pennsylvania he asked
about preaching. They referred him to private worship in the
church that evening.

> A man read in German they [the visiting Methodists] knew not
> what, sung and played upon the *four thousand dollar* organ: sermon
> or prayer they heard not. I doubt much if there is any prayer here,

[12] March 11, 1774; JLFA, I, 110.
[13] August 23, 1776; JLFA, I, 198.
[14] January 15, 1775; JLFA, I, 146.
[15] February 15, 1805; JLFA, II, 460.
[16] October 18, 1774; JLFA, I, 135.
[17] February 17, 1783; JLFA, I, 438; cf. June 7, 1790, p. 642.

public or private, except the stated prayers of the minister on the Sabbath day. But the brethren have a school for boys at Nazareth, and one for girls at Bethlehem; and they have a store and a tavern; the society have worldly wealth and worldly wisdom: it is no wonder that men of the world, who would not have their children spoiled by religion, send them to so decent a place.[18]

It was all too "Dutchified" and neat and satisfied and worldly to please him. Like the churches of the German Lutherans and German Reformed, he counted them

citadels of formality—fortifications erected against the apostolic itinerancy of a more evangelical ministry. Ah! Philadelphia, and ye, her dependencies, the villages of the State of Pennsylvania, when will prejudice, formality, and bigotry, cease to deform your religious profession, and the ostentatious display of the lesser morals give place to evangelical piety? [19]

No fire of the Lord could be expected to break forth from here.

As for the United Brethren, they were very fine indeed. Asbury had asked that Philip Otterbein take part in his ordination. The two were fast friends: "There are very few with whom I can find so much unity and freedom in conversation as with him." [20] Early in his American ministry Asbury met Benedict Swope: "Mr. Benedict Swope, a preacher in high Dutch, came to see me. He appeared to be a good man, and I opened to him the plan of Methodism." [21] When Otterbein, Swope, and Martin Boehm expressed their evangelical zeal in forming their denomination among the Germans, it looked so Wesleyan that these United Brethren were often called German Methodists. Asbury loved them and preached among them. But even these near Methodists were short of expectations. They had the doctrine and they had the piety, but they lacked the discipline. They were always tending to lapse from itinerancy to "locality."

[18] July 20, 1807; JLFA, II, 549-50.
[19] July 22, 1807; JLFA, II, 550.
[20] June 18, 1776; JLFA, I, 190.
[21] January 4, 1774; JLFA, I, 103.

I was informed that proposals were in agitation for settling Mr. Swope, and allowing him a maintenance. But none of these things shall give me much distress. My soul quietly resteth in the Lord.[22]

Came to Antietam settlement, and spoke in a Dutch church: a travelling ministry would be more productive of good among these people; their preachers and people are too fond of *settling,* and having things established on the *regular plan.*[23]

I feel, and have felt thirty-two years, for Pennsylvania—the most wealthy, and the most careless about God, and the things of God: but I hope God will shake the State and the Churches. There are now upwards of twenty German preachers somehow connected with Mr. Philip Otterbein and Martin Boehm; but they want authority, and the Church wants discipline.[24]

Our German brethren of Otterbein's have shouldered us out, but have failed to establish themselves.[25]

At the end of the Baltimore Conference in 1814 the conference members met in the German church and Asbury "discoursed on the character of the angel of the Church of Philadelphia, in allusion to P. W. Otterbein . . . whose funeral discourse it was intended to be." [26] Along with Otterbein they buried the tentative negotiations for a merger of the Methodists with the United Brethren.

It was difficult for Asbury to find anything kind to say about the Baptists. Relations were fairly good in the north, especially in New England, where the Baptists were genteel and inclined to receive the Methodists as fellow dissenters from the Congregational standing order. So on his first episcopal journey to New England in 1791, when he was finding his reception cool enough in Connecticut, he "found a free, open-hearted Baptist minister, who rose from his bed, and received us kindly. . . . His wife is a kind, loving

[22] December 3, 1776; JLFA, I, 206.
[23] May 31, 1786; JLFA, I, 512.
[24] August 1, 1803; JLFA, II, 400.
[25] June 12, 1808; JLFA, II, 572.
[26] March 24, 1814; JLFA, II, 753.

soul; their children obliging, and ready to serve us cheerfully." [27] Next day at New London "the New Light Baptists were very kind, and some of them appeared like Methodists." Baptist churches and homes were often opened to him.

Relations were far from good, however, in the middle states, the south, and the west, where Asbury's preachers and the Baptists were strenuous competitors. Typically there were Baptists present wherever Asbury and the Methodists arrived; there were many of them and they pressed him hard. They multiplied their ministry by the ordination of the most gifted or prominent members of their congregations. These preachers were indigenous; the settlers understood them. Asbury labeled them "John's people." It was hardly safe for the Methodists to go away to conference because "John's people intend to come a fishing about, when we are gone." Asbury named Brother Wyatt "to keep the ground against the Baptists" by circulating among the preaching places while the Methodist brethren were away.[28] "The Baptists show their enmity, and go from house to house persuading weak people to be dipped, and not to hear the Methodists; and they bring their preachers in our absence." [29]

There were some early instances of hospitality and joint work. Over a period of about a year and a half Asbury baptized some converts by immersion out of deference for their wish for the Baptist usage.[30] But the lines were always hardening.

The Lord is graciously working on the hearts of the people at F. Andrews's; but the Baptists endeavour to persuade the people that they have never been baptized. Like ghosts they haunt us from place to place. O, the policy of Satan! Some he urges to neglect the ordinances altogether; others he urges to misunderstand them, or make additions to them.[31]

[27] June 13, 1791; JLFA, I, 680.
[28] April 10, 1780; JLFA, I, 344.
[29] April 8, 1780; JLFA, I, 344.
[30] January 8 and September 24, 1785; June 24, 1787; JLFA, I, 481, 495, 546.
[31] January 17, 1776; JLFA, I, 176.

Here some have been awakened amongst the Methodists, and have joined the Baptists; thus we have laboured, and others reap the fruit.[32]

But what is to be done? Must we instrumentally get people convinced, and let Baptists take them from us? No; we will, we must oppose: if the people lose their souls, how shall we answer it before God? I met with a woman who warmly contended for dipping, as though it had been for life. Another began with me about going to their houses; and said, we must all live in heaven. I said, there will be no rebaptizing there. She said, we must imitate our Lord. I said, our Lord rebuked the wind, and walked upon the sea. The point is this: the Baptists and Methodists came and preached together; our simple young men not knowing how they would act; the people being unacquainted with them, are for receiving both.[33]

Asbury made them choose. Some Delaware people came weeping for fear they would lose Methodist preaching. Asbury said they might have it by providing for houses where the Methodists preached alone. There would be no mixture of the Methodists and Baptists in this case.[34] Evidently the Baptists were wary of the mixture too.

At Wicocon the glory is departed. A few Baptist women stood at a distance and wept, whilst I administered the sacrament: they dared not come to the table, lest they should be discovered by their own people.[35]

As for the North Carolina Baptists, he found them dead and worldly, thus needing Methodist awakening.[36] The Baptists resented proselyting much as others did: "There is a good work of God here; but some of the Baptists rage because we have what

[32] November 12, 1801; JLFA, II, 313.
[33] July 19, 1779; JLFA, I, 305-6.
[34] July 20, 1779; JLFA, I, 306.
[35] December 18, 1785; JLFA, I, 499.
[36] June 22 and 26, 1780; JLFA, I, 359, 360.

they lost; but while we keep close to God, and preach the power of religion, they can do us no harm." [37] Like every post-Puritan critic of Baptists, he found it easy to ridicule their insistence on immersion: "If plunging-baptism is the only true ordinance, and there can be no true Church without it, it is not quite clear that ever Christ had a Church until the Baptists *plunged* for it." [38] "Preaching water" was a favorite charge.[39] So in those areas where the Baptists were friendly, they were dead; in those areas where they were lively, they were wrong. Why anyone would be a Baptist when he could be a Methodist was never clear to Asbury. Perhaps he never tried his best to understand.

One basis for Asbury's suspicion of Baptists was his conviction that there was in them some taint of Calvinism. When he found a Baptist preacher making and selling whiskey, he said, "It is no wonder that those who have no compassion for the non-elect souls of people should have none for their bodies." [40] In a letter to Wesley he told of a Baptist preacher who lived under "Calvinian principles," backslid from God, finally recanted, and tried to publish his recantation but was prevented by his stubborn Baptist colleagues. "Maryland," he said, "does not abound with Calvinism; but in Virginia, North and South Carolina, and Georgia, the Baptists labour to stand by what they think is the good old cause." [41] And if there was any question about the Calvinism of the Baptists, there was no question about the Calvinism of the Presbyterians. Asbury always called the New Englanders by the name of Presbyterians too. Whether they were Scottish, Scotch-Irish, New England Puritan, or Continental Reformed, they were all Presbyterians, and they were all Calvinists.

If there was one thing that infuriated Asbury it was Calvinism! His understanding of what Calvinism was had come from Wesley.

[37] August 7, 1780; JLFA, I, 372.
[38] March 4, 1784; JLFA, I, 458.
[39] July 18, 1779, and September 21, 1780; JLFA, I, 305, 379.
[40] July 25, 1780; JLFA, I, 369.
[41] September 20, 1783; JLFA, III, 30.

John Wesley . . . was the son of parents who held in abhorrence the doctrine of election, especially as asserted in the seventeenth century by Puritan disputants. Wesley himself, while still in Oxford, had come to identify the doctrine of election with the assertion of divine reprobation. . . .

For Wesley this issue was apparently decided as early as 1725. Nowhere in his writings does one find this subject raised again as a matter for further concern or decision. This inadequate and negative feature of Wesley's thought remained characteristic of his assertions on this subject throughout his lifetime. In truth the Pauline affirmation of divine predestination does *not* explicitly demand the corollary of divine reprobation, as, for example, St. Augustine clearly discerned; but for Wesley it did so, and he was not prepared to permit a caveat against his logical decision.[42]

The argument had been hardened to inflexibility by the Anglicans and Puritans before Wesley's time. Wesley and Whitefield fought out their round in the controversy with the same tragic rigidity; once their differences had got into the light of world publicity, each would have viewed any reconsideration as a concession. To make matters worse, just before Asbury left for America, Wesley had deliberately identified Calvinism with antinomianism—irresponsible dependence on some gracious status with God rather than an actual amendment of life and character. When some of his society members were found bubbling over with evangelical grace but living in gross immorality, "Wesley's response to this disheartening development was to charge the societies with theological error rather than moral turpitude." [43] As Wesley phrased it in the Minutes for the London conference of 1770: "We said in 1744, 'We have leaned too much toward Calvinism.' Wherein?" The answers showed the error of claiming that "a man is to do nothing in order to justification." Rather, a man who desires favor with God is to get on in faithfulness, in working for life, in ceasing from evil and learning to do well, in doing "works meet for repentance."

[42] David C. Shipley, "The European Heritage," HAM, I, 33.
[43] *Ibid.*, p. 37.

"And if this is not in order to find favour, what does he do them for?" [44]

Whitefield was dead before this conference, but other opponents were quick to defend God's initiative in justification by faith alone. The resulting controversy gives credit to nobody. Those who championed one event of justification by faith alone did not satisfy Wesley's drive for increasing faithfulness and for getting on to a fullness of the Christian life. Wesleyans, in an attempt to require personal holiness, posed "two justifications."

> Salvation is a process of human living characterized by at least two distinctive theological events (or judgmental declarations of the Almighty) designated the "justifications." One is justified "in the day of conversion" by faith alone based on the imputed righteousness of Christ. This is the first distinctive event marking the initiation of the Christian life. But salvation is at the same time a process culminating in "the justification of the believer in the day of judgment." The explicit condition of this justification is a "faith which works by love," productive of actual goodness through the God-given faith-action of a life lived under the power of a divinely initiated, divinely designed redemptive flow of life. This is the second distinctive event in the process of salvation, marking a final judgment upon the quality of the Christian life. [45]

Theologian John Fletcher produced his *Checks to Antinomianism* presenting the Wesleyan position in its best light.

Asbury came warm from all this Calvinist-Arminian controversy in England to his ministry in America. There was no need to resurvey the issue as he saw it. Wesley and Fletcher were entirely convincing. Indeed, he became convinced that he saw the Wesleyan view in the Scriptures so plainly that he wanted no recourse to Wesley or to any human authority at all.

> We think that among the very best, and greatest human authors who have written *to admiration on the great truths of God, yet have*

written large volumes on different subjects and have made large extracts from other authors, have been led into seeming or real inconsistencies, which might be made use of by their enemies as contradicting some of the great truths of gospel doctrine and order, which they had nobly defended in some of their other writing, and that by oversight, and that we scruple not to say of our great John [Wesley] the divine.

You yourselves having only read his own works think and believe you find some strong Calvinistic expressions in his own writing and doubtless you would find many more if they are not corrected in the fifty volumes of his *Christian* Library extracted from Puritan-Calvinistic writers. Our old Father in the last grand Fletcher controversy was most severely pressed by his Calvinistic opponents on these Calvinistic phrases left in his own works and in the Christian Library.[46]

Asbury could see it all now plainly on the face of the Scriptures without the aid of church fathers, Methodist or otherwise. One wonders if the situation is similar to a study he made of Wesley on Romans wherein he discovered that some thoughts he had long believed were his own were earlier derived from Wesley.[47]

Wherever there was religious lethargy in the New World—and among the nominal and birthright church membership there was much of it—his first thought was Calvinism. He said the Presbyterians cried "The Church! the Church!" but they let their own meeting house go to ruin and "lost the power of religion, if they ever had it." Their congregations were hard for him to penetrate even when he was invited to address them; he felt that the Presbyterians who professed to be Christians were unfaithful and the attenders who made no profession were careless. As for the Presbyterian preachers, they were "too metaphysical and superficial" to offer any remedy.[48]

I had a desire to hear for myself, Mr. Patrick Allison, the Presbyterian minister. His discourse was quite systematical and amusing, but if he

---

[46] Address to the General Conference of 1816; JLFA, III, 533.
[47] March 9, 1780; JLFA, I, 339.
[48] JLFA, I, 17, 83, 439.

had studied to pass by the conscience of his hearers, he could not have done it more effectually.[49]

Came to Canaan, after preaching at a new meeting house. Here naught would satisfy but my going to the ancient Presbyterian church. I reluctantly complied, and made a feeble attempt on Luke xi, 13. I offended, and was offended: the people seemed uneasy and wished to be gone. This is the first, and I expect will be the last time I shall speak in that house, if not in that place. Twenty-five years ago the people in this place had religion; at present, it is to be feared, there is little or none. How it is I know not; but at such places I feel dreadfully,—as if such people were the worst of all under the sun, and at the greatest distance from God.[50]

From thence I came to Halifax. . . . Here some have been brought to God; a few Presbyterians and Baptists lifted out of the Calvinian and Antinomian quicksands.[51]

Wherever there were those who regularly confessed their sins and as regularly waited, under the word, for God's initiative with a gift of grace, he cried "Antinomianism," almost another term for Calvinism as he saw it. How could these preachers be content to let their people believe they were simply dependent on God and his will? This was too passive. The people must repent and believe at once; from this "instrumental cause" of repentance and belief would come the effect of new birth and new life.[52]

Thus do thousands charge God foolishly: "We cannot repent and bring forth fruits meet for repentance; we cannot cease from evil, and learn to do well; we cannot deny ourselves, and take up our cross; we cannot come to Christ that we may have life. At least, we cannot do these things *now;* we must wait God's time." But God requireth these things *now;* therefore, those who say they cannot do them, practically say he is a hard master.[53]

[49] April 2, 1775; JLFA, I, 153.
[50] July 24, 1791; JLFA, I, 689.
[51] To John Wesley, March 20, 1784; JLFA, III, 33.
[52] June 28, 1773, and June 19, 1774; JLFA, I, 83, 119.
[53] November 23, 1777; JLFA, I, 253.

But since that time [first centuries of Christian era], absolute, unconditional predestination has made its way into the Church, which nullifies all laws, human and Divine—for if men cannot do otherwise than they do, why should any law inflict punishment for their crimes? . . . How easily might men, believing this doctrine, ascribe their envy, malice, and most cruel inclinations, to the effect of Divine predestination.[54]

The people here appear unengaged: the preaching of unconditional election, and its usual attendant, Antinomianism, seems to have hardened their hearts.[55]

Wherever there were those who expressed their trust in God in terms of election or perseverance, he preached the terrors of backsliding. He demolished them with his battery of texts insisting on the present assurance of personal conversion and the present yearning after holiness of life. He assumed that any who glorified in God's gracious election had no lively concern with Christian growth.

After preaching, I visited a young man who seemed to be at the point of death: he was full of unbelief, and I fear it was through his Calvinistic notions.[56]

Guyse's paraphrase has lately afforded me great delight. It is a pity that such a man ever imbibed the Calvinistic principles.[57]

I heard the celebrated Mr. Peabody again to-day. He insisted on eternal election; the gift of the Father to the Son; the renewal of the little flock by grace; and the Father's good pleasure; from Luke xii, 32. He detained us two hours; and had many devoted admirers. He spoke to the sinners with great words, but to little purpose.[58]

[54] July 25, 1777; JLFA, I, 244.
[55] June 30, 1781; JLFA, I, 408.
[56] February 24, 1772; JLFA, I, 21.
[57] December 28, 1773; JLFA, I, 100.
[58] September 11, 1774; JLFA, I, 131.

Brother Agee of this neighbourhood had a child of ten years of age, that found the Lord in a gust of thunder and lightning, and straightway preached to all the family: at the same time a poor backslider was cut to the heart; he thought himself to be dying, and cried out against the doctrine of not falling from grace as the means of his fall, and warned those about him of those destructive principles.[59]

Attended quarterly meeting at Morgantown—I spoke on superstition, idolatry, unconditional election, and reprobation, Antinomianism, Universalism, and Deism.[60]

Even if it should be Methodists who were "settling on their lees," he suspected corruption by Calvinism. By some such worldly theology they were being quenched in their passion for holiness. Those who were "hurt with Calvinism" were not easily healed.[61]

As a host of *Journal* entries point out, Asbury really had no aversion to being led or bent to the will of God. An interesting juxtaposition occurs in his entry for July 5, 1774:

In reading the Life of Calvin, it appeared that many, in his day, had opposed the doctrine of predestination; and all who opposed it were spoken of by him and his followers, as bad men. My fever returned this evening, and it was a painful, restless night. But the will of the Lord be done! Though he slay me, yet will I trust him![62]

Concerning his illnesses he always talked like a Calvinist. He certainly believed God had a detailed plan for the ages.

I ended the first volume of Prideaux's Connexions, and had a clear view of the state of the nations at the different periods of the Church of God—a just view of which is highly necessary for the understanding of the prophecies. The revolutions of kingdoms have been wonderful in all ages; and it ought not to be thought strange, if they should be so now. But in all the various turns of Divine

[59] April 21, 1783; JLFA, I, 440-41.
[60] July 24, 1790; JLFA, I, 646.
[61] July 30, 1780; JLFA, I, 370.
[62] JLFA, I; 121.

providence God had, and still has, spiritual ends, and the welfare of his Church, in view.

In reading the second volume of Prideaux, I was struck with the exact fulfillment of Daniel's prophecy "The seventy weeks being divided into three periods,—that is, into seven, sixty-two, and one week.[63]

In connection with biblical prophecy he seemed to accept God's plan with awe and wonder, and to date it quite literally, just as Wesley did. He attempted, indeed, to improve a bit on Wesley. Where Wesley saw the end of the present kingdom of Satan in 1836, Asbury scheduled it for 1808 or 1809.[64] But in graciously converting men to be Christians and maturing them in their faith, God did not elect individually. God's way of operation in salvation was completely plain. It was the Methodist plan.

Wesley knew the long association of Calvinism and evangelicalism in America and it worried him. He had written to the American preachers in 1783:

Undoubtedly the greatest danger to the work of God in America is likely to arise either from preachers coming from Europe, or from such as will arise from among yourselves speaking perverse things, or bringing in among you new doctrines, particularly Calvinism. You should guard against this with all possible care; for it is far easier to keep them out than to thrust them out.[65]

There was no need for his concern in the case of Asbury. One of his early pastoral acts in America was the circulation of Fletcher's *Checks*,[66] which he felt admirably answered all the Calvinists. And a month before Wesley had written to the preachers in 1783, Asbury had sent a letter to Wesley:

I see clearly that the Calvinists on one hand, and the Universalians on the other, very much retard the work of God, especially in Penn-

[63] January 6-7, 1779; JLFA, I, 292.
[64] To Thomas L. Douglass, July 30, 1807; *Methodist History*, October, 1962, p. 40.
[65] To the Preachers in America, October 3, 1783; LJW, VII, 191.
[66] June 28, 1773; JLFA, I, 83.

sylvania and the Jerseys, for they both appear to keep people from
seeking heart religion. . . . I think you ought always to keep the
front of the Arminian Magazine filled with the best pieces you
can get, both ancient and modern, against Calvinism: they may be
read by future generations.[67]

On the American side of the ocean Asbury kept packing large
stores of anti-Calvinist ammunition into editions of the *Discipline*,
which every Methodist was to purchase, "next to the word of
God." [68] When the American version of the *Arminian Magazine*
appeared in 1789, the first article was "A Sketch of the Life of
Arminius" and the second was "An Account of the Synod of
Dort." During the two years of its existence, the magazine was
heavy with the anti-Calvinist theme.

Asbury was not entirely blind to the truth on both sides of the
controversy. His long *Journal* entry for January 26, 1779, is the
classic statement of his wider understanding.

I spent much of my time in reading the third volume of Mr. Hervey's Dialogues. I like his philosophy better than his divinity.
However, if he is in error by leaning too much to imputed righteousness, and in danger of superseding our evangelical works of righteousness, some are also in danger of setting up self-righteousness,
and, at least, of a partial neglect of an entire dependence on Jesus
Christ. Our duty and salvation lie between these extremes. We
should so work as if we were to be saved by the proper merit of our
works; and so rely on Jesus Christ, to be saved by his merits and the
Divine assistance of his Holy Spirit, as if we did no works, nor
attempted anything which God hath commanded. This is evidently
the Gospel plan of man's salvation:—St. Paul says in one place, "By
grace are ye saved, through faith; and that not of yourselves, it is
the gift of God." In another place the same apostle saith, "Work
out your own salvation with fear and trembling." But some, who see
the danger of seeking to be justified by the deeds of the law, turn all
their attention to those passages of Scripture which ascribe our

[67] September 20, 1783; JLFA, III, 30-31.
[68] Preface to the *Discipline*, 1790; JLFA, III, 84.

salvation to the grace of God; and to avoid the rock which they discover on the right hand, they strike against that which is equally dangerous on the left, by exclaiming against all conditions and doings, on the part of man; and so make void the law through faith—as if a beggar could not cross the street, and open his hand (at the request of his benefactor) to receive his bounty, without a meritorious claim to what he is about to receive. What God hath joined together, let no man put asunder.[69]

But it was his mission in America to be a partisan for an enthusiastic Wesleyan view against any whose doctrine had left them only what he called "a form of religion," those who had "lost the power."

We are not ignorant that the Gospel has been preached in the eastern and northern parts of these United States, from the earliest settlement of the country; but this has been done chiefly, though not entirely, through the Calvinistic medium: the consequence of which has been, that the religious books in general which have been circulated in those parts, and in some measure through the southern states, have more or less maintained the doctrines of unconditional election and reprobation—that "GOD is" not "loving to every man," and that "his mercy is" not "over all his works"; and consequently, that "Christ did" not "die for all," but only for a small select number of mankind; by the means of which opinions, Antinomianism has insensibly gained ground, and the great duties of self-denial, mortification, crucifixion to the world, and all the other severe but essentially necessary duties of religion, have been too much neglected and despised. . . .

We desire to guard against all unkind and unchristian reflections nor would we even use the appellation of Calvinist, if it was not for the sake of distinction. Indeed we believe the Calvinistic system has passed its meridian, and is declining in the Christian church.[70]

He records an amazing number of instances when he was shown hospitality in Presbyterian homes and churches: "I must give the

[69] JLFA, I, 293-94.
[70] Preface to *The Arminian Magazine*, April 10, 1789; JLFA, III, 67-68.

Presbyterians the preference for respect to ministers." [71] He did not respond with any hospitality to Presbyterian doctrine. Only once, in the heat of his enthusiasm for the Cumberland camp meetings, did he encourage any real union of Presbyterians and Methodists. In this revival work he really thought the Presbyterians had embraced Methodism.[72] The notion of union died in infancy.

> Friendship and good fellowship seem to be done away between the Methodists and Presbyterians; few of the latter will attend our meetings now: well, let them feed their flocks apart; and let not Judah vex Ephraim, or Ephraim, Judah; and may it thus remain, until the two sticks become one in the Lord's hands.[73]

Occasionally he met overt opposition from resident clergy and laity who opposed him on grounds of doctrine or of order.

> Preached to a very gay congregation, consisting of four or five hundred people: there appears to be a prospect of good among them.
> The priests of all denominations, Dutch and English, appear to be much alarmed at our success; some oppose openly, others more secretly.[74]

By his own account he overcame many a Calvinist in controversy. He intended to get them all.

There are a few instances where Asbury seems to say a word which allows room for his Christian brothers of other denominations. These appear to be mostly private sentiments expressed to his *Journal*.

> I see God will work among Menonists, Dunkers, Presbyterians, Lutherians, Episcopalians, Dutch, English, no matter; the cause belongs to God.[75]

[71] March 29, 1793; JLFA, I, 753.
[72] October 20-21, 1800; JLFA, II, 257-58; JLFA, III, 197, 199, 201, 221, 230, 233, 239, 249, 261; HAM, I, 525-29.
[73] August 19, 1806; JLFA, II, 515.
[74] August 8, 1782; JLFA, I, 432.
[75] August 19, 1782; JLFA, I, 431.

I see a difficulty in saying anything of any denomination of people—it is so much like evil speaking to mention their faults behind their backs: I will avoid it, and endeavour to prevent others doing it in my presence.[76]

But his long-range intention is plain: the other groups are to cooperate until they have seen the rightness of the Methodist doctrine, discipline, and practice. The genuine Christians in other groups are really Methodists placed out of context by some miracle of God.

Met with a man to-day who came from a place about eighteen miles from the springs. He never heard a Methodist before, nor saw one; yet he appeared to be a Methodist in principle, experience, and practice. He was brought to the knowledge of himself and of God by the means of sore afflictions of body, prayer, and reading. Thus we see the Lord works where, and in what manner he pleases.[77]

The choice is whether the others will become Methodists one by one or by group decision.

Many people attended this evening, to hear an account of the rise, discipline, and practice of the Methodists; on which subject I enlarged with a warm exhortation, and had great liberty and satisfaction.[78]

After the various duties of the day, I met the society, and showed them the utility of our economy, the advantages of union and the fearful end of leaving our fellowship.[79]

The death of Mr. Dickenson was something remarkable: full of the world, and judge of Caroline County court; he went to bed well, was taken in an hour after, and soon took his departure out of this to the unseen world. He was often heard to speak against the Methodists; he knows now the truth of these things we controvert.[80]

[76] November 6, 1784; JLFA, I, 471; cf. pp. 305, 310.
[77] August 8, 1776, JLFA, I, 196; cf. pp. 242, 320, 427.
[78] January 27, 1774; JLFA, I, 104.
[79] July 31, 1774; JLFA, I, 126.
[80] October 26, 1779; JLFA, I, 318.

Preached at Isaac Layton's: called to warn my brethren against the poisonous and false principles of opposing sectarists. I was doing only what it was my bounden duty to do, and, indeed, acting on the defensive.[81]

I lamented the gayety of the children of Methodists; but yet they do not appear to be so full of enmity against God and his people as other children.[82]

Asbury's logic and that of his denominational opponents often failed to engage at all. They were aiming words at each other as each scrambled, more or less successfully, for some share in the enterprise of enlisting Americans. It was Asbury's efficiency in administration and revival which overcame. Methodism really was superior in the terms most Americans understood best: "It will be best for us not to strive, nor cry, or cause our voices to be heard! our increase will be known, and our success will be seen enough to raise envy." [83]

[81] December 13, 1780; JLFA, I, 393.
[82] September 19, 1787; JLFA, I, 550.
[83] To Daniel Hitt, January 21, 1804; JLFA, III, 277.

PART IV

Turning Loose

16
END OF THE ROAD

When Francis Asbury was sixty-six he said, "I wish the connection to do as well without me as with me, before they must do without me. I fret like a father, that wishes to see his children married and settled before he dies."[1] The image is a good one. As one biographer puts it:

> American Methodism had been the puling infant of evangelical religion when he landed in Philadelphia in 1771; it was now a lusty youngster whose holy bawling had been heard from the Atlantic to the Mississippi, and from Canada to the Gulf of Mexico.[2]

Methodist numbers were exceeded only by the Baptists. And the hardest thing Father Asbury had to do was to turn loose his child.

Asbury had been unique as the father of American Methodism. He regarded himself as unique; no other man was so well prepared as he to guide the American Methodists. Strawbridge, Rankin, O'Kelly, Lee, Coke, and Wesley had felt the force of his correction.

[1] To Thomas L. Douglass, July 11, 1811; *Methodist History*, October, 1962, p. 49.
[2] Herbert Asbury, *Methodist Saint*, p. 285.

The Methodist people regarded him as unique; as he had symbolized the connection, he now symbolized the denomination. Even the turbulent democrats among the preachers knew where the authority lay until they should have the strength to change matters. Now Asbury and Methodism faced one of the great problems of uniqueness—succession. How could there be a replacement for the man who was admittedly one of a kind?

The question could not be dodged. Asbury's health was most precarious. The marvel is that he ever lived to reach the age of seventy. Ever since that first winter ride in the New World he had been a kind of ambulatory invalid. In 1794 he could not cross "the American Alps," and had to give long-distance direction to the western preachers; in January and February of the following year he was incapacitated at Charleston. Then, in 1797, the bad situation became worse. Asbury started out to meet the preachers in the Western Conference but was forced to return. "From the 9th of *April* to the 27th of *May* I have kept no journal. The notes of our travels and troubles taken by Jonathan Bird and Joshua Wells, will tell a small part of my sorrows and sufferings. I have travelled about six hundred miles with an inflammatory fever, and fixed pain in my breast." [3]

On June 10 he arrived in Baltimore, and lodged at the home of a Methodist about a mile from the city. There he "lounged away a week in visiting." He tried to preach the following Sunday, and mourned that he could talk but fifteen minutes. His friends put him back to bed and showered him with kindness, but he cried out that he was a "worthless lump of misery and sin," unworthy of so much attention. So he was again carried into Baltimore, where he tottered happily about among the sinners and the Methodists, preaching, praying, and organizing. [4]

For several months of 1798 he was reduced to comparative inactivity, too weak and sick even to read or study. Three physicians,

[3] April 6, 1797; JLFA, II, 127-28.
[4] Herbert Asbury, *Methodist Saint*, p. 287.

called into consultation in 1799, advised that he give up preaching altogether.[5] In that year he curtailed his episcopal work somewhat; only six conferences were appointed. Asbury talked of resigning as bishop at the General Conference of 1800. "I am more than ever convinced of the propriety of the attempts I have made to bring forward Episcopal men." [6] He would probably have died of chagrin if the preachers had agreed to replace him.

The subject of help for Asbury was not new to the General Conference. From the time of his first episcopal tour with Henry Willis in 1785, he had customarily had a traveling companion to share the work of preaching, administration, and presiding.

McKendree had accompanied him in 1792; while in 1790 Whatcoat had with him crossed the mountains into the new territory, and had shared his hardship and all but tragic adventures. Lee and Roberts and Hull had gone with him about New England, and no journey had ever been made to the Southwest without companionship.[7]

In 1798 and again in 1799 there appeared a note in the Minutes: "Jesse Lee travels with Bishop Asbury." This was the record of a sort of official chaplaincy designed, if circumstances required, to free Asbury from all work except the ordinations and the stationing of the preachers. Lee could ride ahead to hold the conferences, following Asbury's sickroom instructions about the preachers.[8]

The General Conference had tried to ease matters in 1796; both Asbury and the conference members seem to have expected that one or more bishops would be elected that year. However, before the maneuvering to present an acceptable candidate was complete, Dr. Coke offered his own services full time in America. Asbury seemed enthusiastic about the proposed arrangement, but declined to give Coke any real power at all. He kept the whole

[5] June 2; JLFA, II, 195.
[6] September 23, 1797; JLFA, II, 133.
[7] DuBose, *Francis Asbury*, pp. 174-75.
[8] Lee, *Short History*, pp. 252-53.

enterprise in his own hands, just as he had always done. Coke complained that Asbury made a mere preacher of him, never consulted him about any episcopal decision, and would not even give him a copy of the list of stations of the preachers of the Georgia Conference after every traveling preacher present was allowed one! Said Coke: "I then saw the will of God concerning me—that I ought not to labour in America." [9]

In 1800 the General Conference tried again to relieve Asbury of some of his load. Once again the maneuvering for the proper candidate began. When the vote was cast, it was a tie between Jesse Lee and Richard Whatcoat. Asbury refused to advocate the election of Lee, and the malicious rumor was that he did not want Lee elected; later the rumor was tracked to another source.[10] On the second ballot Whatcoat was elected by a margin of four votes. Now Whatcoat was hardly one year younger than Asbury and hardly one whit healthier. He had few gifts for administration— which may have been just as well, because Asbury kept firm grip on all the operation of the church anyway. The two old men lovingly limped across the republic; Whatcoat shared the preaching but Asbury made the decisions. Asbury's health actually improved so that he outlived his younger colleague and in 1806 was alone on his rounds again. Bishop Coke, now married to a rich and pious widow, again offered to return to America full time if the land, the work, and the authority were actually divided between him and Asbury. The Americans agreed that no situation was desperate enough to justify this; they declined Coke's offer.

Asbury then made quite a fuss about the awful loneliness of his eminence and the likelihood that he would die before an adequate successor would be elected.

I have only to say I sit on a joyless height, a pinacle of power, too high to sit secure and unenvied, too high to sit secure without divine aid. My bodily and mental powers fail, I have a charge too great

---

[9] To the New York Conference, January 6, 1806; JLFA, III, 334-39.
[10] Leroy Lee, *Life of Jesse Lee*, pp. 376-78.

for many men with minds like mine. I hope not to jump down, fall down, or be thrown by haughty ambition, but I mean to step down as soon and safely and completely as I can; and not to stand alone, but break the fire by having more objects than one. . . .

When a man is in his 62 year it is not safe to trust a great work to his trembling hands. A president of a state of the states ought to know when to retire for fear of damages, and if heaven would insure my life, bodily and mental powers, would heartily advise my brethren to provide immediately for such a charge! and not to rest it with me, or any one man upon earth.[11]

He tried for an emergency electoral committee to elect another bishop between conferences in 1807, but this plan was defeated in Virginia, probably because Jesse Lee led the opposition.[12] Not until the General Conference of 1808 did he get his episcopal cohort. William McKendree had come to the height of his powers in his duties on the western frontier. McKendree's appearance was rough as he entered the Baltimore pulpit to fill his appointment to preach to the General Conference, but his sermon pierced the assembly. After hearing him Asbury is reported to have said: "That sermon will make him a bishop." When the election came, McKendree had a large majority on the first ballot. Asbury was hearing less acutely when the conference stated that the bishops should be equal. He made a note in his *Journal* about "electing dear brother William M'Kendree assistant bishop." [13]

As he went out from that General Conference to his tours he rejoiced, "The burden is now borne by two pairs of shoulders instead of one; the care is cast upon two hearts and heads." [14] This time he was right. And the power must pass from his hands to those of his successor. For over twenty years there had been no effective will but Asbury's in the making and sending of Methodist preachers. Now this must be shared with another and finally given to another.

[11] To Thomas Haskins, October 17, 1806; JLFA, III, 356.
[12] Lee, *Short History*, pp. 348-49.
[13] May 8, 1808; JLFA, II, 569-70.
[14] *Ibid.*

McKendree must have been a very patient man. He saw that the Methodist Episcopal Church had grown so large that he must counsel with a "cabinet" of the presiding elders in order to make wise appointments, and he courteously but firmly resisted Asbury's pressure to make him operate in the old way. Under McKendree's leadership the conferences began to handle their business with dispatch. At the General Conference of 1812 McKendree pointed up his chief concerns at the opening of conference with a brief episcopal address. As the address closed Asbury was on his feet in protest: "I have something to say to you before the conference." Now they stood face to face. "This is a new thing. I never did business in this way, and why is this new thing introduced?" McKendree broke the tension with a right reply: "You are our father, we are your sons; you never have had need of it. I am only a brother, and have need of it." [15] While McKendree did not hesitate to change the episcopal procedures, he was not zealous to make Asbury conform to the new. Asbury attended the conferences when he could and he shared fully in stationing the preachers.

So Asbury went on and on. Nobody took seriously his talk about resigning, least of all himself. He had been traveling constantly for well over forty years. On the road was his identity, his authority, his constituency, his family, his sickbed. His companions tended the sick man along the road; when it appeared he was unfit even to be carried, the home of the nearest Methodist was hospital enough. In spite of his constant complaining, Asbury did not intend either to be coddled or to be left behind.

> I would not be loved to death, and so came down from my sick room and took to the road, weak enough. Attentions constant, and kindness unceasing, have pursued me to this place, and my strength increases daily. I look back upon a martyr's life of toil, and privation, and pain; and I am ready for a martyr's death.[16]

[15] Robert Paine, *Life and Times of William McKendree* (Nashville: Southern Methodist Publishing House, 1869), I, 263-64.

[16] July 19, 1814; JLFA, II, 756.

If he could walk twice across the sickroom he declared himself
fit for the road. He could not go home because he had none; the
road was his home so he kept going. The thing a bishop did at the
end of one tour was to start another. By Asbury's definition, if
he stopped he was no bishop.

> It would be a disgrace to our episcopacy, to have bishops settled on
> their plantations here and there, evidencing to all the world, that
> instead of breathing the spirit of their office, they could, without
> remorse, *lay down their crown*, and bury the most important talents
> God has given to men! [17]

He was an itinerant to the end.
  Increasingly he became a traveling exhibit of Methodism.

> During the last few years of Asbury's life his travels through
> the domain of Methodism were triumphal processions. He was by
> now the best-known man in the United States, and wherever he
> went great crowds assembled to see him and hear him preach; he
> was entertained by mayors and governors, and when he visited a
> capital city during session of the legislature, he was invited to address
> the statesmen. . . . Methodists throughout America, contemplating
> the results of his labours, regarded him with awe and veneration, and
> it was not uncommon for a congregation to burst into tears as he
> tottered or was carried into a church.[18]

All the people he had visited before expected him to visit one
more time for a farewell; all the people he had not visited insisted
that he come now before it was too late.

> They keep me busy: I must preach; I am senior; have long been
> absent; some never expected to hear me again; possibly, I may never
> come again: I am reminded that such and such I dandled in my
> lap: the rich, too, thirty years ago, would not let me approach them;
> now I must visit them and preach to them; and the Africans, dear,
> affectionate souls, bond and free, I must preach to them.[19]

[17] *Discipline*, 1798, p. 44.
[18] Herbert Asbury, *Methodist Saint*, p. 300.
[19] April 11, 1810; JLFA, II, 635.

Friends advised him to take care of himself and told him he was making his rides too long. "Yet they will scarcely be denied when invited to their houses, making my rides longer still." [20] At one place he had a marriage, a funeral, and a baptism—and remarked, "Well; make the best of me whilst you have me; it will not be often." [21] All the while he was getting death notices of his old friends and was preaching their funerals. At the grave of Henry Willis he said:

Rest, man of God! Thy quiet dust is not called to the labour of riding five thousand miles in eight months,—to meet ten conferences in a line of sessions from the District of Maine, to the banks of the Cayuga,—to the States of Ohio, of Tennessee, of Mississippi,—to Cape Fear, James River, Baltimore, Philadelphia, and to the completion of the round. Thou wilt not plan and labour the arrangement of the stations of seven hundred preachers; thou wilt not attend camp meetings and take a daily part in the general ministration of the word; and often consume the hours which ought to be devoted to sleep, in writing letters upon letters! Lord, be with us, and help us to fulfill the task thou hast given us to perform! [22]

As always in his case, when his ability to work became limited and the authority was not firmly in his own hands, the old uneasiness came back to haunt him. Locality, marriage, Presbyterian government, and Calvinism all snowballed into one towering threat in his thinking and destroyed much of his peace. His mind would ramble from the heights of joy in contemplating the multiplying Methodists to dark suspicion and despair.

We have amongst us, numbers local and travelling preachers, men that are Presbyterians in church government; and Presbyterianism governs the new world. Baptists, Independants, and all are one. Give the people a choice, and the preachers liberty to station themselves. [23]

[20] October 27, 1814; JLFA, II, 762.
[21] October 15, 1815; JLFA, II, 794.
[22] August 11, 1813; JLFA, II, 740.
[23] To Thomas L. Douglass, September 29, 1815; *The Western Methodist*, April 25, 1834; *Methodist History*, October, 1962, p. 56.

We lament that men should leave the traveling line. I lament that before they have left, their hearts have left it; then they want to be Presbyterians in government, choose for themselves, and bargain with the people. Apostolic Methodism is too pure, which they want to change. Artful in craft, they say, too much power, too many overseers to watch our conduct and report us; let us make and appoint our rulers first; then set them aside, and rule ourselves in a great degree.[24]

Ah! have I lost the confidence of the American people and preachers? or only a few overgrown members, that have been disappointed; and the *City lords,* who wish to be Bishops, Presiding Elders, and Deacons, and reign as Kings without us,—*over us.* . . . I am only Vice-President.[25]

He could shout:

But whether health, life, or death, good is the will of the Lord: I will trust him; yea, and will praise him: he is the strength of my heart and my portion forever—Glory! glory! glory! [26]

But he could yearn after some assurance of his own place, and cry:

Alas! what a little have I done—what a little have I suffered? Me! who am less than the least of all saints, not worthy to be called preacher, much less a bishop and an apostolic successor. I want to live, to make the best of a poor day's work.[27]

Finally the old man wore out completely. In 1813 he wrote his views about episcopacy in a long address to McKendree, he wrote his valedictory to the presiding elders, and he wrote his will.

[24] To Jacob Young, August 2, 1815; *Methodist History,* October, 1962, p. 59.
[25] To Thomas L. Douglass, August 20, 1812; *Methodist History,* October, 1962, pp. 51-52.
[26] October 22, 1815; JLFA, II, 794.
[27] To Thomas L. Douglass, December 20, 1811; *Methodist History,* October, 1962, p. 50.

Knowing the uncertainty of the tenure of life, I have made my will, appointing Bishop M'Kendree, Daniel Hitt, and Henry Boehm, my executors. If I do not in the meantime spend it, I shall leave, when I die, an estate of two thousand dollars, I believe: I give it all to the Book Concern. This money, and somewhat more, I have inherited from dear departed Methodist friends, in the State of Maryland, who died childless; besides some legacies which I have never taken. Let it all return, and continue to aid the cause of piety.[28]

In October of 1815 he gave up the last of his episcopal responsibility to McKendree.

My eyes fail. I will resign the stations to Bishop M'Kendree—I will take away my feet. It is my fifty-fifth year of ministry, and forty-fifth year of labour in America. My mind enjoys great peace and divine consolation.[29]

His only commission now was his own conviction that he should do as much good as he could. He was determined to attend the South Carolina Conference at Charleston, but did not make it; he changed his aim toward the General Conference in Baltimore to meet in spring of 1816. This plan failed too. The last entry in his *Journal* is for December 7, 1815: "We met a storm and stopped at William Baker's, Granby."

[28] June 6, 1813; JLFA, II, 732-33.
[29] October 22, 1815; JLFA, II, 794.

CONCLUSION

After the last entry in his *Journal*, Bishop Asbury lived nearly four months. He actually arose from that bed at Granby in South Carolina and set out for Baltimore in his carriage. He endured his consumption, gigantic blisters which he constantly applied in the name of medicine, and complications of bronchitis and influenza. Along the way his friends would carry him into churches where he would preach pitifully rambling but touching sermons. The last of these was at Richmond, Virginia, in March of 1816. He insisted that his friends carry him into the old Methodist church. There he sat on a table and preached from Rom. 9:28, "For he will finish the work, and cut it short in righteousness: because a short work will the Lord make upon the earth." After a day of rest he ordered the entourage back onto the road to head for Fredericksburg. At George Arnold's home in Spottsylvania he collapsed, and this is where he found rest.

It was on a Sunday, October 27, 1771, that Francis Asbury landed in America; it was on a Sunday, March 31, 1816, that he died. He had recognized that it was church time and had just done his best to join in the Arnold family worship. John Wesley Bond read the appointed lectionary passage for the day, Revelation 21, which begins:

And I saw a new heaven and a new earth: for the first heaven and the first earth were passed away; and there was no more sea. And I John saw the holy city, new Jerusalem, coming down from God out of heaven, prepared as a bride adorned for her husband. And I heard a great voice out of heaven saying, Behold, the tabernacle of God is with men, and he will dwell with them, and they shall be his people, and God himself shall be with them, and be their God. And God shall wipe away all tears from their eyes; and there shall be no more death, neither sorrow, nor crying, neither shall there be any more pain: for the former things are passed away.

Asbury was about to take up his mite fund book and ask for contributions for the poor missionary preachers, but they reminded him that there were none present except the family.[1]

First he was buried in the Arnold family cemetery. There were funeral services in many places; one of the most memorable was conducted in St. George's Church in Philadelphia, April 23, 1816, with Ezekiel Cooper preaching from the same text—II Tim. 3:10 —Asbury had used to preach Wesley's funeral twenty-five years before: "But thou hast fully known my doctrine, manner of life, purpose, faith, longsuffering, charity, patience." When the General Conference met in May of 1816, arrangements were made to remove his body to Baltimore. On May 10, 1816, a funeral was held in Baltimore, with a company of some twenty thousand to escort his remains to a vault beneath the pulpit of the Eutaw Street Church; all Methodist congregations in Baltimore heard funeral sermons the following Sunday. Thirty-eight years later his body was removed once more to Mount Olivet Cemetery in Baltimore, where many noted Methodists were already interred.

No biographer should try to make him lovable, for this he would never allow himself to be. But no honest student of Asbury can escape a kind of awe. One awful fact is his commission as he saw it; another is the way he never let it go.

[1] Letter of John Wesley Bond to William McKendree, April 1, 1816.

Bibliography

Francis Asbury did not especially want a biography. He thought his *Journal* would be quite enough. The truth is that the *Journal* is not only enough; it is too much. So there is excuse for a biography to abbreviate and to interpret more concisely. But the reader who wants the more substantial Asbury will do best to go directly to the *Journal* and to Asbury's letters.

The *Journal* was available in part before Asbury's death and has been published in various editions since his death. The *Journal* and letters are available now in convenient form in the three-volume set published by Abingdon Press in 1958; this set has earned some criticism for incomplete bibliography and for poor transcription of the letters, but it is adequate for most users. Most references to Asbury's *Journal* and letters in this book are cited to this 1958 edition; direct quotations from it are identified by date as well.

If the reader wants Asbury biography, only two works are really noteworthy. One was written by Ezra Tipple, who loved Asbury and the Methodists; one was written by Herbert Asbury, who pretended to despise them. Those who seek a biography with a special concern for church polity and for the succession of conferences may want to consider DuBose.

Those who want to feel the cyclic nature of Asbury's travel may go the rounds year by year with Smith. Those who especially want Asbury the hero may supplement Tipple with Duren. Only special students of Asbury are likely to get to the rare-book rooms for Strickland or for Mains.

When the reader wants Asbury in a broader context of Methodist history, let him go to the three-volume *History of American Methodism* published in 1964. Asbury is a dominant figure in Volume I, and his contribution is weighed by experts. The bibliographies in this *History* will open the researcher's way to its predecessors, from the more recent works of Sweet back through Stevens, Bangs, and Lee. Tigert's *Constitutional History* bears up exceedingly well; Tigert displays both a vigor of style and impressive knowledge. Drinkhouse, as a Methodist Protestant, shows Asbury critically and laments what a true democrat he might have been. In many ways Lee's *Short History* is the most delightful of them all and gives a fine feeling of contemporaneousness.

Since the early history of the Methodists in America interlinks so closely with the life of Asbury, the *Minutes* and *Disciplines* up to the year 1816 become documents of his biography. Five printed volumes are especially valuable. The first is a compilation entitled *Minutes of the Methodist Conferences Annually Held in America, from 1773 to 1794, Inclusive*. Beyond 1794 the reader must turn to *Minutes of the Annual Conferences of the Methodist Episcopal Church*, Vol. I. If original copies of the *Disciplines* are lacking, one finds the five earliest reprinted in pamphlets about 1887 by Charles Nutter. The student of Asbury will soon want to proceed to *The Doctrines and Discipline of the Methodist Episcopal Church in America. With Explantory Notes by Thomas Coke and Francis Asbury*, which is the *Discipline* for 1798. For the General Conferences, the most helpful compilation is *Journals of the General Conference of the Methodist Episcopal Church, 1796-1836*. The careful listing of *Journals, Minutes*, and *Disciplines* on pages 699-701 of the first volume of *The History of American Methodism* helps to assort the mixture of titles and editions.

Periodical literature on Asbury is disappointing. The two volumes of the *Arminian Magazine* (Philadelphia, 1789-90) are quickly mined. Periodicals published after his death make references enough to Asbury, but they tend to idealize him or to perpetuate questionable anecdotes. Instead of illuminating some new facet of Asbury's life and thought, the popular magazine articles usually repeat a biographical formula and attach a moral. *Methodist History* and *World Parish*, its predecessor, rendered good service by publishing letters of Asbury discovered since the 1958 edition of the *Journal* and letters.

In the midst of documentary riches on Asbury one dares to hope for discovery and careful publication of more information, especially about his youth. It is unfortunate to have an impression circulating that Asbury was romantically attached to a girl in England when the two shreds of evidence cited are altogether inconclusive (the letters to his parents of October 26, 1768, and June 7, 1784). It is equally unfortunate to have Asbury's apprenticeship associated with service at the "Old Forge" without some careful qualification. Briggs offers no evidence for this conclusion and his bare assertion leaves other biographers somewhere short of certainty.

Following is a selected list of materials for the inquiring reader; it includes the items cited in these comments.

The Arminian Magazine. 2 vols. Philadelphia: Printed for John Dickins by Prichard and Hall, 1789 and 1790.

Asbury, Francis. *The Causes, Evils and Cures of Heart and Church Divisions, Extracted from the Works of Mr. Jeremiah Burroughs and Mr. Richard Baxter.* Philadelphia: Hall, 1792; New York: Lane and Scott, 1849.

———. *Extracts of Letters Containing Some Account of the Work of God Since the Year 1800. Written by the Preachers and Members of the Methodist Episcopal Church to Their Bishops.* New York: Cooper and Wilson, 1805.

———. *A Selection of Hymns from Various Authors, Designed as a Supplement to the Methodist Pocket Hymn-Book.* New York: Wilson and Hitt, 1808.

Asbury, Herbert. *A Methodist Saint: The Life of Bishop Asbury.* New York: Alfred Knopf, 1927.

Bangs, Nathan. *A History of the Methodist Episcopal Church.* 4 vols. New York: Mason and Lane, 1838-41.

———. *The Life of Freeborn Garrettson; Compiled from His Printed and Manuscript Journals and Other Authentic Documents.* New York: Emory and Waugh, 1830.

Barton, Jesse Hamby. "The Definition of the Episcopal Office in American Methodism." Unpublished Ph.D. dissertation, Drew University, 1960.

Boehm, Henry. *Reminiscences, Historical and Biographical, of Sixty-Four Years in the Ministry.* Ed. by Joseph Wakeley. New York: Carlton and Porter, 1865.

Briggs, Frederick W. *Bishop Asbury: A Biographical Study for Christian Workers.* London: Wesleyan Conference Office, n.d.

Bucke, Emory Stevens, ed. *The History of American Methodism.* 3 vols. Nashville: Abingdon Press, 1964.

Carroll, Grady L. E. *Francis Asbury in North Carolina.* Nashville: Parthenon Press, 1965.

Carroll, H. K. *Francis Asbury in the Making of American Methodism.* New York: Methodist Book Concern, 1923.

Cartwright, Peter. *The Autobiography of Peter Cartwright.* Centennial Edition. Nashville: Abingdon Press, 1956.

Clark, Elmer T. *An Album of Methodist History.* New York and Nashville: Abingdon-Cokesbury Press, 1952.

Clark, Elmer T.; Potts, J. Manning; and Payton, Jacob S., eds. *The Journal and Letters of Francis Asbury.* 3 vols. Nashville: Abingdon Press, 1958.

Coke, Thomas. *Extracts of the Journals of the Late Rev. Thomas Coke.* Dublin: Methodist Book Room, 1816.

———. *Substance of a Sermon Preached . . . at the Ordination of the Rev. Francis Asbury.* London: J. Paramore, 1785.

Cooper, Ezekiel. *The Substance of a Funeral Discourse on the Death of the Rev. Francis Asbury.* Philadelphia: Jonathan Pounder, 1819.

Dickins, John. *Friendly Remarks on the Late Proceedings of the Rev. Mr. Hammett to Which is Annexed a Letter Addressed to Himself.* Philadelphia: Parry Hall, 1792.

Dimond, Sydney G. *The Psychology of the Methodist Revival: An Empirical and Descriptive Study.* Nashville: Whitmore and Smith, 1926.

The Doctrines and Discipline of the Methodist Episcopal Church in America. With Explanatory Notes by Thomas Coke and Francis Asbury. 10th ed. Philadelphia: Printed by Henry Tuckniss, sold by John Dickins, 1798.

Drinkhouse, Edward J. *History of Methodist Reform, Synoptical of General Methodism 1703 to 1898 with Special and Comprehensive Reference to Its Most Salient Exhibition in the History of the Methodist Protestant Church.* 2 vols. Baltimore and Pittsburgh: Board of Publication of the Methodist Protestant Church, 1899.

DuBose, Horace M. *Francis Asbury; A Biographical Study.* Nashville: Publishing House of the M.E. Church, South, 1909.

Duren, William L. *Francis Asbury; Founder of American Methodism and Unofficial Minister of State.* New York: The Macmillan Company, 1928.

Emory, John. *A Defence of Our Fathers and of the Original Organization of the Methodist Episcopal Church Against the Rev. Alexander M'Caine and Others.* 5th ed. New York: Mason and Lane, 1840.

Feeman, Harlan L. *Francis Asbury's Silver Trumpet; Nicholas Snethen.* Nashville: Parthenon Press, 1950.

Garrettson, Freeborn. *The Experience and Travels of Mr. Freeborn Garrettson.* Philadelphia: Printed by Parry Hall, published by John Dickins, 1791.

Gewehr, Wesley M. *The Great Awakening in Virginia, 1740-1790.* Durham: Duke University Press, 1930.

Jackson, Thomas, ed. *The Lives of Early Methodist Preachers, Chiefly Written by Themselves.* 6 vols. London Wesleyan Conference Office, 1865.

Jarratt, Devereux. *The Life of the Reverend Devereux Jarratt, Rector of Bath Parish, Virginia, Written by Himself in a Series of Letters Addressed to the Rev. John Coleman.* Baltimore: Warner and Hanna, 1806.

————. *Thoughts on Some Important Subjects in Divinity in a Series of Letters to a Friend.* Baltimore: Warner and Hanna, 1806.

Johnson, Charles A. *The Frontier Camp Meeting, Religion's Harvest Time.* Dallas: Southern Methodist University Press, 1955.

Journals of the General Conference of the Methodist Episcopal Church, 1796-1836. New York: Carlton and Phillips, 1855.

Kilgore, Charles. *The James O'Kelly Schism in the Methodist Episcopal Church.* Mexico City: Casa Unida De Publicaciones, 1963.

Larabee, William C. *Asbury and His Coadjutors.* 2 vols. Cincinnati: Swormstedt and Poe, 1854.

Lee, Jesse. *A Short History of the Methodists in the United States of America*. Baltimore: Magill and Clime, 1810.

Lee, Leroy M. *The Life and Times of the Rev. Jesse Lee*. Louisville: Published by John Early for the Methodist Episcopal Church, South, 1848.

Lewis, James. *Francis Asbury*. London: Epworth Press, 1927.

McLean, John. *Sketch of Rev. Philip Gatch*. Cincinnati: Swormstedt and Poe, 1854.

Mains, George. *Francis Asbury*. New York: Eaton and Mains, 1909.

Marsden, Joshua. *Poems on Methodism Embracing the Conference or Sketches of Wesleyan Methodism: and American Methodism, A Plea for Unity by an American Methodist*. Philadelphia: Sorin and Ball, 1848.

Minutes of Several Conversations between the Rev. Thomas Coke, LL.D., the Rev. Francis Asbury and Others, at a Conference Begun in Baltimore, in the State of Maryland, on Monday, the 27th of December, in the Year 1784. Composing a Form of Discipline for the Ministers, Preachers and other Members of the Methodist Episcopal Church in America. Philadelphia: Printed by Charles Cist, 1785. [This is the first *Discipline;* in the Charles Nutter reprint the other four *Disciplines* through 1789 are bound with it.]

Minutes of the Annual Conferences of the Methodist Episcopal Church, Vol. I, 1773-1828. New York: Mason and Lane, 1840.

Minutes of the Methodist Conferences Annually Held in America, from 1773 to 1794, Inclusive. Philadelphia: Printed by Henry Tuckniss, sold by John Dickins, 1795.

Minutes of the Methodist Conferences from the First, Held in London, by the Late Rev. John Wesley, A.M., in the Year 1744. Vol. I, 1744-1797. London: John Mason, 1862.

O'Kelly, James. *The Author's Apology for Protesting Against the Methodist Episcopal Government*. Richmond: John Dixon, 1798.

————. *A Vindication of the Author's Apology with Reflections on the Reply*. Raleigh, N. C.: Joseph Gales, 1801.

Outler, Albert, ed. *John Wesley*. New York: Oxford University Press, 1964.

Paine, Robert. *Life and Times of William McKendree, Bishop of the Methodist Episcopal Church*. 2 vols. Nashville: Southern Methodist Publishing House, 1869.

Peters, John L. *Christian Perfection and American Methodism.* Nashville: Abingdon Press, 1956.

Phoebus, William. *Memoirs of the Rev. Richard Whatcoat.* New York: Joseph Allen, 1828.

Pilmoor, Joseph. Manuscript Journal, the Historical Center Library, Old St. George's, Philadelphia. Transcription by Cornelius Hudson.

Sherman, David. *History of the Revisions of the Discipline of the Methodist Episcopal Church.* New York: Nelson and Phillips, 1874.

Smith, George G. *Life and Labors of Francis Asbury.* Nashville: Publishing House of the M.E. Church, South, 1898.

Snethen, Nicholas. *An Answer to James O'Kelly's Vindication of His Apology.* Philadelphia: S. W. Conrad, 1802.

———. *A Reply to an Apology for Protesting Against the Methodist Episcopal Government.* Philadelphia: Henry Tuckniss, 1800.

Spellmann, Norman W. "The General Superintendency in American Methodism, 1784-1870." Unpublished Ph.D. dissertation, Yale University, 1961.

Sprague, William B., ed. *Annals of the American Pulpit: Commemorative Notices of Distinguished Clergymen.* Vol. VII. New York: Robert Carter and Brothers, 1861.

Stevens, Abel. *History of the Methodist Episcopal Church.* 4 vols. New York: Carlton and Porter, 1864-67.

Strickland, William P. *The Pioneer Bishop, or the Life and Times of Francis Asbury.* New York: Carlton and Porter, 1858.

Sweet, William Warren. *Methodism in American History.* Revised ed. Nashville: Abingdon Press, 1954.

———. *Religion on the American Frontier, 1783-1840, Vol. IV: The Methodists.* Chicago: University of Chicago Press, 1946.

———. *The Rise of Methodism in the West: Being the Journal of the Western Conference, 1800-1811.* New York: Methodist Book Concern, 1920.

———. *Virginia Methodism.* Richmond: Whittet and Shepperson, 1955.

Telford, John, ed. *The Letters of the Rev. John Wesley A.M.* 8 vols. London: Epworth Press, 1931.

Thrift, Minton. *Memoir of the Rev. Jesse Lee, with Extracts from His Journals.* New York: Bangs and Mason, 1823.

Tigert, John J. *A Constitutional History of American Episcopal Methodism.* 6th ed. Nashville: Publishing House of the M. E. Church, South, 1916.

Tipple, Ezra Squier. *Francis Asbury, The Prophet of the Long Road.* New York: Methodist Book Concern, 1916.

Upham, Francis. *Old John Street Methodist Episcopal Church.* New York: Central Publishing, 1932.

Wakeley, J. B. *The Heroes of Methodism: Containing Sketches of Eminent Methodist Ministers and Characteristic Anecdotes of Their Personal History.* New York: Carlton and Porter, 1856.

Ware, Thomas. *Sketches of the Life and Travels of Rev. Thomas Ware.* New York: Mason and Lane, 1839.

Watters, William. *A Short Account of the Christian Experience and Ministereal Labours of William Watters, Drawn up by Himself.* Alexandria, Va.: S. Snowden, 1806.

Wesley, John. *The Journal of the Rev. John Wesley.* Ed. by Nehemiah Curnock. 8 vols. London: Epworth Press, 1938.

————. *The Letters of the Rev. John Wesley A.M.* Ed. by John Telford. 8 vols. London: Epworth Press, 1931.

————. *A Plain Account of Christian Perfection.* London: Epworth Press, 1952.

————. *Primitive Physic.* 27th ed. New York: Hitt and Ware, 1814.

————. *The Works of John Wesley.* Ed. by Thomas Jackson. 14 vols. Grand Rapids: Zondervan, 1958.

Wilkins, Henry. *The Family Adviser.* 5th ed. New York: Hitt and Ware, 1814.

Wood, A. Skevington. *The Inextinguishable Blaze.* Grand Rapids: Eerdmans, 1960.

Index

Abingdon, Md., 51, 124-27
Account of the Primitive Church, King, 47, 166
African Methodist Episcopal Church, 185
African Methodist Episcopal Zion Church, 185
Albany, N.Y., 73
Alexandria, Va., 72
Allegheny Mountains, 72, 73
Allen, Richard, 185
Allison, Patrick, 197-98
Allowances, 104, 107
Anglicans, 42, 109, 113, 187-88, 195: in colonies, and problem of sacraments, 39, 43; *see also* Church of England
Annapolis, Md., 38
Antietam settlement, 191
Antigua, 52
Antinomianism, 159, 195-96, 198-99, 200, 203
Apostolic order, 171-74
Appalachian Mountains, 73
Arminian Magazine, 132, 133, 202
Arnold, George, death of Asbury at home of, 219-20
Asbury, Elizabeth Rogers, 15, 16, 106
Asbury, Francis: to America, 13-14, 20; and American Revolution, 32-41, 89, 116; apprenticeship, 15-16; birth, 14-15; celibacy, 105-6; death, 219-20; education, 15, 19; as General Assistant, 44-45, 48-51; illnesses, 76-77, 200, 210-11, 214-15; medical practices, 76-77; on Methodist superiority, 14, 112, 186-206; in New York, 23-26, 30; ordination,

Asbury, Francis—*cont'd*
51-53; parents, 15, 16; in Philadelphia, 20, 23, 30-31; preaching in England, 18-20; under Rankin, 28-31; reading, 19, 36, 140-41; religious awakening, 16, 17; religious intensity, 139-48; in south (1772-73), 26-28
—as bishop, 54, 56-57: antislavery attempts, 176-82; autocracy, 144-45; Book Concern work, 134-36; controversy over conferences and power of episcopacy, 58-67; and episcopacy, 165-75; hymnal compiled by, 131-32; letter writing, 108-9, 116; money raising, 104-5; and Negroes, 182-85, 215; polity building, 95-110; preaching, 80-94; schools founded, 124-31; symbol of Methodism, 209-18; traveling, 71-79; writing and editing, 131-32
Asbury, Joseph, 15
Asbury, Sarah, 15
Augusta, Ga., 183

Backsliding: Asbury's preaching against, 85, 87, 158, 162, 199
Baker, William, 218
Baltimore, 24, 57, 72, 73, 90, 119, 120, 219: Asbury's circuit at, 27, 28, 30, 31, 113; Asbury's funeral and burial in, 220; Asbury's visit of 1797, 210; Christmas Conference of 1784, 50-52; Cokesbury College in, 127-28; General Conference of 1792, 63-65; segregation at Lovely Lane Church, 184